# Story or Be Forgotten

*In a World Obsessed With Noise, Story Is Survival.*

Théo Mahy-Ma-somga

Published by Artist Lab Editions

ISBN: 979-8-9989036-6-3

First Edition – 2025

*To Papi and Mamie. For the love, the roots, and the strength. You were the quiet force behind it all.*

# Summary:

*"Let them call you mad. They never heard the rhythm you were dancing to. That was never the point. Change the lens, watch the story change."*

–T

# How to Read This Book

This book is built like a manifesto, raw, personal, strategic. It's both a declaration and a guide. You'll find reflections, frameworks, and lessons drawn from real experiences. Each chapter is designed to give you clarity, momentum, and a sense of direction. But beyond the ideas, this is a book meant for action.

That's why at the end of the book, you'll find a full section dedicated to exercises, practical tools to help you integrate everything you've just read. These exercises are not optional. They are here to turn knowledge into transformation.

There are two ways to read this book:

1.  You can pause after each chapter, take your time, reflect, and go directly to the related exercises before moving forward. This is ideal if you want to build gradually, step by step.

2. Or you can power through the entire book first, let the energy of the words carry you, and once you've reached the end, go back, and dive deep into the exercises with a fresh, global view of the journey.

There is no right or wrong way. The only rule is: don't just read, use it. This isn't just a book. It's a toolkit, a mirror and a spark.

Now, it's yours.

# A Word From The Author:

They told you: speak smart, stay clean, keep it tight. Trade your truth for applause, dim your fire for the light.

Smile like you mean it, pitch like you care. But strip out the soul, and no one is there.

You followed the script, you colored inside. Hide the chaos, the grief, the rage you denied.

Now you're polished, you're perfect, you're ready to sell. But you vanished so quietly, no one could tell.

This isn't about branding, or playing it cool. It's not about frameworks or following rules.

It's the sound of your blood when it hits the page. It's the myth you reclaim when you step out of the cage.

So bury the fake, and speak like you bled. Or stay silent forever, and count yourself dead.

Because likes won't remember, and reach doesn't feel. But a story that cuts? That's how you stay real.

# Foreword:

# The New Renaissance

Creativity is Renaissance. Not a gentle pursuit of beauty or self-expression, but a clash of ideas, a crucible of transformation. Every masterpiece, every groundbreaking concept, every disruptive innovation is born from conflict. Conflict with norms, with expectations, with your own limitations.

The world is flooded with noise, mediocrity, and imitation. Most creators drown in it, thinking their talent alone will save them. It won't. Talent is the entry ticket. Strategy is the game. And those who master both don't just survive, they redefine the landscape.

This book is not for the casual creator. It's for those willing to transcend their craft, tell their story and wield it like a weapon. It's for those who understand that in this era, you don't just need to create, you need to inspire. You need to place the story at the center of the dialogue.

To inspire, you must think differently. Act differently. It's about accepting to show yourself, as you are, not creating an image that looks good. You must be willing to break what others are too scared to touch. You are here because you feel it, the pull. The urge to stand at the center of the creative ecosystem, not as another voice, but as a force of nature.

Story or Be Forgotten. Because today, story is no longer something we tell at night to fall asleep. It's not a soft whisper. It's not decoration. It's not content. Story is a verb. It moves. It strikes and rewrites the air around us. It's action, raw, emotional, deeply encoded in our DNA. To "story" is not to perform, but to reveal. Not to polish, but to pierce. Story is the act of opening the truth we've buried to survive.

If you fake it, you will be forgotten. If you perform, they'll scroll past. If you cheat the story, the story will erase you.

Because story will last. The algorithm won't.

Let's start by acknowledging something simple: if you're still standing today, that's already something to be proud of. This world didn't prepare us for what we've had to endure. No one gave us a manual. No one showed us how to adapt to the chaos we're living in. We had to figure it out on our own. Quietly and that was brutal.

Did you feel it? That slow, silent pain of trying to keep up, of reshaping yourself just to function? The world is full of noise. It moves fast. It overwhelms. And most of us are still wondering where to look, where to go, and who we're supposed to be in all this. We didn't sign up for this pace, for this pressure. Taking a breather is a start. It's necessary, but it's not enough.

That doesn't mean rejecting the tools of our time. Quite the opposite, use them and learn from them. Surf the wave of change instead of resisting it. Technology is not the enemy, disconnection is. There's no going backwards. This is the world now.

But to move through it without losing yourself, you need an anchor. That anchor is your story. If we want to move forward, not just survive, but belong, to do so we have to use our story. Every day. Not as a performance, but as a tool. We use it to seek connection where we've grown distant. We use it to rebuild bridges the world has burned. And we use it to return to ourselves, piece by piece, word by word.

This manifesto is your blueprint. It will teach you to harness your art, your mind, and your influence to build something that cannot be ignored. The world doesn't need another artist. It needs a new breed of creators, those who understand creativity as both an art and a strategy.

Welcome to the New Renaissance.

I know what it feels like. The doubts. The fire. The moments when you wonder if you're crazy for wanting more, for wanting to create something that actually matters. You're not crazy. You're exactly where you need to be.

I didn't believe I was capable of anything. I wanted to believe it, but all I could see was the world conspiring against me. I hadn't checked the right boxes. I grew up in a social housing project in the south of France. For the first decade of my life, my reality was made of concrete blocks, of an easygoing rhythm designed to keep me where I belong. Outside our project, houses rose on the hills, each one bigger than the last, looking down on us. And I kept asking myself: why are we so different? Why can't I live there? Disclaimer: I live in one of those houses now. But I'm not telling you this to brag or to prove that you can rise from the bottom. I'm telling you because for years, I didn't believe I could. I didn't have a father, but I had a remarkable grandfather. My mom wasn't always present, but my grandmother was nothing short of exceptional. And still, doubt was always there. It still is, even now, as I write. I wrestle with my own demons, the ones that whisper I'm not supposed to be here.

That I'm not allowed to take a pen and share stories.

But you know what? Hell yes, I am. And so are you. The world is loud. It knows how to tap into your deepest fears and show you exactly what you want to keep hidden. It took me a minute, maybe a lifetime, to realize I was worth it. But now? I refuse to let my fears, my stories, my judgments, my visions, my beliefs, or any noise that fills the void, hold me back. We all carry a story. We all carry our baggage. But I had the desire to change mine. To disrupt the script the system had written for me. That's what you're reading here. My honest attempt. My humble gift. Everything I needed to hear is here. It's precious to me. This is life. And I want you to make the most of it.

I'm not here to lecture you. I'm here to walk this with you. To show you what I've learned, the hard way, and to help you move faster, stronger, sharper. You already have the spark. Together, we'll turn it into something unstoppable.

You're not just another artist.
You're a force in the making.
Let's make sure the world knows it.

Théo

Juin 2025

# Introduction:

The world has never moved so fast. Scary for some? Maybe. Deeply engaging for others. Opportunities now hide behind every door, at the other end of every call, within every conversation.

Despite what the headlines scream, the world, yes this one, is better than it has ever been. And sure, there's still work to be done. Plenty. But overall, we are moving in the right direction. This era wasn't built against you. It was built for you. For the artist within you.

You may not feel that way. You might even doubt that artist exists. But it does. You do. You possess a creative soul, buried deep maybe, but extraordinary, persistent, and real.

The problem? If only there were just one. We don't know where to start. We don't know what to do. We're frozen. Scared. Unsure. Watching everyone else move faster than us.

We are facing a crisis of collective consciousness. And to succeed, whatever success means to you, you'll need to step away from the mob.

How much information have you already consumed today? Your brain is constantly activated. That could be a gift, given we still tap into only a fraction of its potential. But the question is: what is your mind being activated by? And for what purpose?

Not long ago, our ancestors received news by word of mouth, weeks or months after events had occurred. It gave them time. Time to process, to feel, to reflect. In cities, information traveled faster, but even then, it allowed space to respond, and to adapt.

Each new wave of discovery brought shifts. Small ones at first, then deeper. Patterns started forming, then accelerating, until we reached the frenzy of now. Books, radio, television, the industrial revolution, the conquest of new frontiers, all of it reshaped our relationship to knowledge. And still, we adapted.

It was a soft evolution. Some resisted. Some feared. But most moved forward because the world felt better. Progress was tangible. Life was evolving. And for the most part, we were keeping up.

Then, the internet came along. And with it, a shift unlike anything humanity had ever seen. The internet was a revolution. An upside down slap in the face. Suddenly, gathering, understanding, and processing information became not just faster but overwhelming. The web connected us to the entire world in a single instant. Opportunities multiplied. But so did the complexity of navigating them.

The more we connected, the harder it became to process correctly, to discern, to find stillness in the flood. We began living in a permanent flux. A permanent noise. To survive, we had to implement parental controls, time limits, and mental walls. The internet was a miracle, but like all revolutions, it came with its casualties.

We lost a part of the population that couldn't adapt fast enough. We witnessed a rise in emotional shutdown people frozen like overloaded screens, unresponsive to reality. Around us, friends, family members, acquaintances, many didn't live long enough to see where it was all heading.

And then came the final blow: social media.

Today, we are not just connected. We are bombarded. Solicited every minute by devices smarter than us, built to capture our attention, to hack our dopamine, to reprogram our desires. We lost another part of the population to this invisible tide. But more importantly, we lost something inside ourselves: stability.

Today, we can't talk about politics anymore because true debate is dead. We buy compulsively, gathering objects we don't need, simply because taking the time to question is too exhausting. We perform to impress people we don't even know, while they are doing exactly the same. We smile on camera, cry backstage. The flood of information hit our brains so abundantly, so brutally, that many of us simply shut down. Even the strongest among us, even the brightest, have crossed dark waters, periods with no breathing room, no clarity, no exit.

But here's the good news. I believe we have a dual green light in front of us. First, we are living in incredible times. Maybe every era thought the same, but I can only speak from what I know. And I know that we will emerge stronger. We are smart animals. And once we rewire properly, we will embrace this complexity and make it serve us, not crush us.

Second, and more importantly for you and me, this is by far the best era ever for creators. By embodying the artist as a mindset rather than a hobby, by understanding that there are strategies and frameworks that work, we are stepping into a field of opportunities like no generation before us ever knew. And there are enough opportunities for everyone. We are in competition only if we think in one dimension. Beyond that, we are allies. You don't have to be smarter. You don't have to be more talented. You don't have to be touched by some higher power. You just need to understand the new game. Your success does not take anything away from mine. Your success is my success. That is what makes this moment so rare, and so powerful.

That being said, we have tools to learn. And a mindset to embody. If you are here, you are probably looking for answers. I won't hand you answers on a plate. Instead, I will share with you what I have worked on, what I have tested, what I have seen work, not just for me, but for everyone around me. This is a recipe. And as my grandmother used to say: once you have the recipe, make it your own. That is exactly what I want you to do here. Adapt. Try. Innovate. Make it yours. Stay within the framework, and watch the magic unfold.

However, I won't lie to you. This won't be simple. This is not something you apply sporadically. It's a mindset. A way of life. A conscious choice. If you are truly seeking greatness, if you are ready to dedicate your energy to it, then stay with me. You won't need to work eighty hours a week to make it happen. But you will need to fully commit to the task at hand. To be present. To be fierce. To be alive. Let's start your artistic revolution.

# Chapitre 1:

# The Creative Strategist

What does it mean to be a creative strategist? It means wearing two hats simultaneously: that of the visionary and that of the tactician. It means being both the innovative, caring, intuitive mind and the strategic, business-oriented force that knows how to move ideas into the real world. Both dimensions exist deep within us, whether we recognize them or not, and if one side feels uncomfortable or unfamiliar, the good news is that we are not trapped by our initial wiring. We have mental models to guide us, cognitive strategies to expand our thinking, and a full panel of tools at our disposal to create the outcomes we are seeking.

In this chapter, we will dive into the real rules of the game, those that go beyond raw talent, and uncover what it truly means to remain not just relevant, but dominant, in today's ever-shifting world. In the second part, we will focus on the single most essential mental model every creative strategist must master, and by the end of this chapter we will explore the unique blend of art, technology, and psychology that lies at the heart of the creative strategist's mindset. From there, you will have a clear method to build and refine a strong creative vision, along with exercises to turn your insights into real action.

## The Rules of the Game

As I mentioned in the introduction, the world today evolves at light speed. We are no longer just encouraged to reinvent ourselves; we are almost forced into it. I remember my grandmother telling me that when she was in school, she chose to become a teacher, and she remained one for forty-five years. No pivots. No reinventions. A single, clear trajectory that shaped her entire professional life. Today, by the time you graduate, the job you picked is probably already obsolete. Entire industries rise and collapse within a decade. Skills that were rare yesterday become common commodities today. What was unthinkable just a few years ago suddenly becomes mainstream and expected. Understanding this reality is not optional anymore. It is the foundation for properly positioning yourself in a world that rewards speed, adaptability, and reinvention.

Your talent alone is not enough. Of course, it matters, it is the first spark, the essential ignition, but it is only the beginning. You must also accept the necessity of continuous evolution, of relentless questioning, of rebuilding yourself again and again without losing your essence.

At the center of the creative strategist's framework lies a single, unchanging word: art. But art is not one fixed thing. It is different for everyone. Painting, music, filmmaking, these are obvious forms of art. But so are design, architecture, even cooking. Anything that merges passion and mastery, anything that channels an internal vision into an external form, belongs to the domain of art. If you're an entrepreneur, this is for you, you are creative at full speed.

That is why we are all creative in our own way. Art is not defined by the medium you use; it is defined by the energy, the intentionality, and the depth you pour into what you build. It is the collision point where passion meets skill, and where what you dream transforms into something others can experience. What you dream of, what you create, must be what resonates most deeply within you. Not what the audience demands. Not what your family expects. Not what the latest trends dictate. What matters is what is truly yours, what you carry in your blood, whether the world is ready for it or not.

If you could bleed your art, what would be in your veins? That is the only real question you need to ask yourself. The only compass that truly matters. Too often, I see creatives sacrificing the very thing that makes them extraordinary, chasing after what's fashionable, what's momentarily applauded, what seems safer. They dilute their uniqueness. They trade their originality for temporary approval, for fleeting attention.

Stop that. Stop it now. You were not built to imitate. You were built to create.

I know this because I've been there. I wrote screenplays that sold, but first, a lot of screenplays that didn't sell at all. Because I was lying to myself. I was horrible at writing horror screenplays. But "hey, there's a niche," they said. Not mine. I wasn't writing from a place of truth. And the worst part wasn't just that I knew it, it was that the person on the other end, the one holding the checkbook, could see it too.

You might think you can fake your way through, perform just well enough to convince others, but you can't. Authenticity isn't a marketing slogan, it's a currency. Your story matters and is your selling card. And everyone can feel it when it's missing.

If you're a painter, don't create another Banksy-style stencil just because it looks cool. Unless it's genuinely yours, and if it is, then make it unforgettable. Make it so alive, so raw, so unmistakably personal that no one could confuse it with anything else, the way Mr. Brainwash once did. It's not imitation, it's homage. It's transformation. Don't imitate the surface of what inspires you. Own its essence and transform it. Otherwise you will not only be forgotten, you won't even be seen.

Quentin Tarantino once said that art is copying and making it better. He was right, your goal is to aim for that. Reinvent what moves you, and twist it. Break it open, then rebuild it into something only you could have imagined. Even a simple carbonara dish can become a work of art if you care enough to elevate it beyond the ordinary.

Art isn't a hobby. It never was. And yet, every day, kids are told that art is something secondary, something "nice" but not essential. Meanwhile, we spend millions visiting exhibitions of dead artists, honoring talents we failed to recognize when they were alive. We love art in all its forms, yet we distrust those who choose to live for it. Why? Because their commitment reminds us of our own compromises.

We dismiss those who choose art as a calling because deep down, we are afraid. We don't take ourselves seriously enough. We hide behind easier narratives, convincing ourselves that practical paths are safer, that dreams are indulgent distractions. But the truth is, we fear what it would cost to take the leap ourselves.

I repeat, art isn't a hobby. It's a way of life. And yes, it's different. It demands that you embrace your difference, even when it isolates you. Especially when it isolates you. Because being different is not a weakness, it is the only way to create something truly meaningful. Are you a misfit? A marginal? Good. You just won the lottery.

I was an awkward kid. I grew up too fast and was always a little too tall for my age. I never really fit in. I was good at school, but I wasn't interested in what they taught. While others focused on the rules, I questioned them. I challenged the status quo while most people prepared for ordinary lives. I wasn't exactly bullied, but I wasn't often included either. And truthfully, I didn't care. I was busy building stories in my mind and doing my own thing.

Art is more than a job. It is an extension of your being, a mirror of your inner world made visible and real. It's how you leave a trace that lasts. It's how you create meaning in a world drowning in noise. We are the living representation of what we create. Our work is an extension of ourselves, a mirror of our beliefs, our struggles, our visions.

And while there was a time when a creation could speak entirely for itself, when the work alone was enough to define the creator, that time has passed. In today's hyperconnected, hypercompetitive world, you must do more. You must embody your art with every fiber of your being. You must become the undeniable proof that what you have built is real, that it comes from a place no algorithm could manufacture, no trend could engineer.

## You are the brand.

During one of our weekly team briefs, I shared
a feeling I couldn't shake. Watching how the
world is evolving, it's becoming clearer every
day, we're heading toward a reality where the
individual is the business. A world of creators,
consultants, experts, and personal brands.
Why? Because many of the jobs that exist today
won't exist tomorrow. It's not just about
having a nice website anymore. That's
outdated. What people look for now is the face
behind it all. The person with a voice, and a
soul.

The Story.

Pulling from my own experience, I am the
brand, arms and legs. I'm the writer. I'm the
creative. I'm the founder who shows up with a
specific voice, a unique way of doing things,
and a distinct energy I bring to my niche. But
that doesn't mean acting all alone, on the
contrary, it's knowing how to build strong
personas around yourself, minds that take you
to the next level and embrace your vision, it's

not about being a chef but being a leader, with an open door, behind which everyone gets inspired. That's not just a role, it's a superpower. And guess what? You have one too.

You are the brand. The brand is you. Why? Because the talent is you. There is no separation anymore, no protective veil between the creator and the creation. Everything you do is a reflection of who you are, and everything you are feeds back into what you create. And here's the hard truth: talent alone isn't enough anymore. It never really was. You cannot simply create and wait. You cannot afford to sit back, hoping that someone somewhere will stumble upon your work, recognize your brilliance, and carry you across the finish line. That dream belongs to another era. Today, you must stay in motion. You must forge your own path deliberately and courageously, not the path others have paved for you, but the one that only you can walk.

You have to become your own brand, with your own story, not a polished, hollow version of yourself designed to please or conform, but a living, breathing, relentless presence. You must be both the work and the worker, the idea and the execution, the vision and the proof.

And yes, that's where the fear kicks in. Right? Good. That's a good sign. Fear means you're standing at the edge of something real. It means you are about to do something that matters. Something that carries risk, and therefore meaning. You will overcome it. You will walk through it, step after step, even when the ground feels uncertain beneath you. You will emerge stronger on the other side, not in spite of the fear, but because you dared to face it. It will be scary at times. It's supposed to be. If it weren't, it wouldn't be worth it.

The great thing, and let me reassure you, is that there are more resources and opportunities available today than ever before. In becoming fully yourself, there is no place to hide, and that's a good thing. Hide from what, anyway?

You are not that important in the eyes of others, and that's liberating. No one out there is sitting in judgment of you. If they are commenting, criticizing, or laughing, they are not truly thinking about you: they are wrestling with their own fears, their own mortality, their own inability to act.

Regardless of who or what frightens you, there is really only one way to fail.
It is not by being criticized.
It is not by being imperfect.
It is simply by not doing it at all.

Inaction is the real failure. And ironically, it rarely provokes judgment or criticism, only silence. A silent void, filled by the heavy weight of missed opportunities and unrealized potential. We will return to this point later, because it is crucial but for now, let's focus on what the world currently offers you: endless possibilities, powerful creative strategies, and the means to seize and transform opportunities into something that truly matters.

I am not asking you to become the next influencer.
I am asking you to become an expert in what you do. An expert in your story or be forgotten.

Is it writing romance novels?
Crafting thriller screenplays?
Painting like Pollock, or developing a revolutionary tool for baby diapers? It doesn't matter what your field is. What matters is that you master it. You must become the expert, the reference, the creator who cannot be ignored. And today, at your fingertips, you have everything you need to make your creations known. In a single click, you can showcase your work to the world.

Do it.

In a single conversation, you can blend your knowledge with decisive insights and build something meaningful.

Do it.

Action is the crucial factor for differentiation.
Action is what separates those who dream
from those who leave a mark. It's not about
being the loudest. It's about being the most
committed. Yes, the world is saturated. Yes, the
noise is real.
And in the next chapter, we will dive into the
art and science of being seen but before we go
there, you must understand something
fundamental: you cannot stay hidden. You
must share your work, and must let it breathe
in the world.

Technology is your best ally, not your enemy.
Today, we are fortunate enough to have tools
that previous generations could never have
imagined.

My grandfather used to walk ten kilometers to
go to school, and ten kilometers back home. No
technology. No shortcuts. He had time to
think, yes, but he didn't have the means to
conquer anything beyond his immediate
reality. His circumstances were what they

were. Today, ours are different. Today, we are equipped to build, to connect, to amplify our vision beyond what any single life could have reached in the past.

It's up to us to seize it.

Even if you are working full-time, raising three kids, and managing everything alone without external help, there is still a window for you to create and share your work. You might not see it immediately, and I am not here to pretend that it is easy. It's not. But it exists, and what you are lacking is not time or ability; it's simply the understanding of how to find and use that space.

You are worthy of everything you desire to build. Your creativity knows it. The strategy you are learning knows it. And if today you are dedicating energy to owning your craft but not to sharing it, then the real challenge is not technical, it's psychological. You are standing in front of a barrier, and you are about to overcome it.

## Mental Models

We live surrounded by systems, systems we rely on every day, yet strangely enough, we often resist them. We avoid structure, process, and strategy, sometimes instinctively, because deep down we fear that rules will cage our freedom. But the right systems don't limit your creativity; they protect and amplify it.

Let me give you an example. Take desires. Seneca famously said that desire is the root of all evil, and in many ways he was right. Desires can entrap us, distract us, scatter our focus. And yet, they also drive us forward. They fuel ambition, innovation, love, and creation. The real question is not whether desire is good or bad, it is whether you are creating meaningful desires, or being consumed by hollow ones.

If desire is what drives us, then what saves us?

Love. Meaning. Connection.

These are the forces that anchor us, that give shape to our work beyond the ego. When you create, when you share, when you build something for others to experience, you are seeking connection. And if you want that connection to be real, you must first connect deeply with the people you are trying to reach.

The psychology of a creative strategist has two faces. One face turns inward: understanding your own mind, your fears, your strengths, your blind spots. The other face turns outward: understanding how people think, decide, and respond to the world around them.

To master this second face, you must become aware of cognitive biases. These are not tricks or manipulations; they are the hidden structures that shape human behavior. They are natural shortcuts that our brains use to make decisions faster, and as a creator and strategist, you have the right, and the responsibility, to understand and use them wisely.

Think like a master chess player. Every piece on the board serves a purpose. Every position, every move, every opportunity is there for a reason. Nothing should be random in your strategy.

Earlier, I told you it was essential to position yourself as an expert, as a leading voice in your field. That's not just branding advice. It's rooted in human psychology: people naturally follow those they perceive as authorities. They are more likely to trust, to agree with, and to support someone they recognize as a leader.

The same principle applies to similarity and belonging. If people see you as "one of them", someone who shares their values, their dreams, their struggles, they are far more likely to connect with you. If your story resonates with them, they will follow you. These psychological principles are not optional, they are fundamental to building real influence. And you must use them. Everything around you, your story, your skills, your positioning can and should become a strategic advantage.

This is exactly how consultants grow businesses from nothing. They offer "only three spots left," creating scarcity, which instantly raises urgency and desire. A marketer with just 500 followers launches a limited offer: twelve spots at twelve hundred dollars per month. Within days, they go from zero clients to twelve, from zero dollars to fourteen thousand in monthly revenue.

Artists have exactly the same opportunities. Whether you have ten paintings, twenty pieces of jewelry, or a series of designs, you can create limited editions, announce drops, open waitlists. "Only eight left." The psychology is the same. The impact is real.

Familiarity. Trust. Confidence. Anticipation. Commitment. These are not marketing gimmicks. They are human fundamentals. And as a creative strategist, you must know them by heart, and use them with precision.

By understanding and studying how the world operates, you will always stay one step ahead, rather than two steps behind. That's not just an advantage; it's a discipline you must consciously cultivate over time. It's a way of observing, analyzing, and integrating patterns so that you can move with the current, instead of fighting against it blindly.

## The Blend of Art, Technology and Psychology.

A creative strategist leverages all three, art, technology, psychology, as pillars to build something real and lasting. But there's one more cardinal point to master: story, and its reflex execution.

What is it that you are offering to the world? Your value proposition doesn't have to be revolutionary or unprecedented. It doesn't have to shock anyone. It simply needs to be clear, purposeful, and articulated with enough precision to resonate.

For example, a writer might say: "I specialize in genre movies that isolate settings to emphasize social commentary, especially the evolving relationships between men and women today."

It's simple and specific. It places the creator exactly where they need to be, in the mind of whoever reads or hears it. Or take another example: a friend of mine in New York started working with Mikey's stuffed toy before it even became a trend. His purpose, through his art, was to give childhood memories a second life, transforming nostalgia into something tangible and meaningful. People were intrigued immediately. They connected emotionally, without the need for elaborate explanations.

I'll say it again: your story doesn't have to be complicated. It simply has to be yours.

Let me take my own example. The "Studio" creates satirical fiction based on true stories, offering deep commentary on societal issues. Our "Campus" provides artists with a platform to connect, to learn the inner workings of the industry, and to position themselves for success. The "Editions" branch publishes screenplays because we believe in the enduring power of words and we know that screenwriting deserves a place on every bookshelf, right alongside novels and essays.

Alright, enough about us. The point is, we didn't reinvent the wheel. We simply held our ground and stood firmly for what we believe in.

The artist has visions. And while you might survive for a time without selling any vision, that won't last forever. Vision is what carries you through the storms. It's what gives your work longevity, relevance, and direction. Execution must be ruthless. What matters is showing up consistently, organizing your actions, and building momentum deliberately.

That brings us to the conversation around hard work versus smart work. It's something I hear often these days: "Work smarter, not harder." And while there's truth in the idea, it's incomplete. In reality, you have to work hard first to find the path to smart work. It's through effort, trial, failure, and iteration that you discover what's truly efficient. You have to pay the price of exploration before you can master optimization.

Hard work is the gateway.
Smart work is the reward.
And once you reach a place of mastery, it won't even feel like hard work anymore. That's why telling someone who's just starting out to "just be smart about it" is poor advice. It skips the essential phase of growth through disciplined effort.

You must be sharp.
You must be organized.
You must think and act strategically at every step.

When you integrate and embody everything we've discussed so far, art, technology, psychology, vision, execution, you won't face blank canvas syndrome or writer's block. You won't sit paralyzed in front of your work. On the contrary, you'll be overwhelmed with ideas, energy, and possibilities. Your plan, once established, becomes your map. A map you trust, consult, adjust when needed, but never abandon. It's the structure that liberates your creativity, not the opposite.

The Creative Strategist is not simply an artist, nor just a thinker or a doer, they are all three at once, blending story, execution, and strategy into one continuous and deliberate movement. They understand that vision, no matter how bold or inspired, is worthless without execution to give it form, and that execution itself, no matter how relentless or tireless, remains blind and chaotic without a strategic framework to guide it.

They don't wait passively for inspiration to strike them like a lightning bolt; they actively create the conditions where inspiration is invited, nurtured, and multiplied. They don't just produce endlessly, throwing work into the void and hoping for the best, they position their creations carefully, aligning their output with their deeper purpose. They don't merely work harder, exhausting themselves for the sake of movement; they build structures, systems, and environments that allow their efforts to accumulate and expand over time.

In this world, talent alone is not enough. Hard work without a clear direction leads inevitably to exhaustion, while intelligence without committed action leads to stagnation and frustration. True creative power lies in the ability to merge these forces, art, technology, and psychology into a seamless and self-reinforcing system that not only adapts to the world but reshapes it along the way.

This is not a hobby.
This is not a weekend side project.
This is a full way of life.

And if you truly embrace it not just in theory, but in daily, relentless practice, the world will not merely notice you; you will carve new spaces into the world itself, forcing it to respond to what you have built.

Now that you understand the foundation, it's time to move forward. What does it truly mean to live as a creator, not occasionally, but fully?

What habits, what routines, and what mindsets separate those who dream idly from those who wake up and build, every single day?

Welcome to The Creative Lifestyle.

# Chapter 2:

# A Creative Lifestyle

Understanding the right mindset is one thing. Putting it into motion to achieve real results is another. To set yourself firmly on the right path, you must accept, right here, right now, that the beliefs you currently hold about your life will be challenged. Not gently, but decisively. Growth demands it.

You have to design a lifestyle that truly aligns with what you're seeking. There's no secret formula, but it is absolutely non-negotiable. Maybe the way you've lived until now has been fulfilling. Maybe you've already felt the undercurrent pushing you toward change. Either way, from this point forward, the rules will be different.

Remember this principle: your life mirrors your standards. Not your goals. Not your dreams. Your standards. It is the expectations you set for yourself, day in and day out, that shape your reality. If you aim for creative excellence, your daily life must become a reflection of that pursuit. Where your attention goes, your energy inevitably follows. With your vision clear in your mind, it's time to align your actions so that success becomes not just possible, but inevitable.

Before we dive deeper, let me share an anecdote that perfectly captures this truth.

A few years ago, I decided to take up tennis. Most of my friends played, and I wanted to be able to keep up with them. To improve, I worked with a coach who taught me every foundational move necessary to hit the ball correctly. Each week, he layered on new elements: watch the ball, move your torso, lock your feet, don't jump, don't fall behind, bounce lightly when your opponent strikes, follow through high above your shoulder, don't rush.

At first, it felt overwhelming. For every single shot, I had a checklist running through my mind. It seemed excessive, almost discouraging. But the lesson was clear: every detail mattered. Mastery wasn't about talent alone; it was about creating the right conditions, consistently.

Over time, instinct took over. What once felt mechanical became second nature. The corrections faded into intuition. My body knew the dance without conscious thought.

Building a creative lifestyle works the same way. There are countless moving parts to consider, countless nuances to refine. Some you may grasp easily. Others will feel unnatural at first. But with persistence, they will embed themselves into your daily rhythm, until the habits of greatness are no longer things you do, but reflections of who you are.

Now, without further delay, let's dive in.

## The Power of Structured Action

One cold evening in March 2015, I was riding my bike across the Williamsburg Bridge in New York City. It was dark, freezing, and I remember reeking of cigarettes, my head pounding, struggling to catch my breath just a few minutes into the climb. I was miserable, out of shape, slightly overweight, completely disconnected from my body. How did I end up there? I used to be active. I played high-level basketball. I worked out all the time. And now, I couldn't even make it across that bridge without falling apart. The truth is, I had forgotten myself. I had just landed my first real job in a studio. I was working on every production I could. And when I wasn't working, I was out drinking, smoking, testing whatever drugs I could get my hands on to stay awake. And every time I wanted to work out, I found a great excuse not to. I had to work. I had to sleep, at least a little. I had to "make it." I was lying to myself, not consciously, but because the wrong motivations were running my life.

That night, on the bike, something cracked. I decided to go back to the drawing board and rewire my daily life to finally serve me. I had the job. I had the social life. I had the love stories, if that's the best way to describe them. But I didn't have a personal life. Out of the four cardinal points, one was missing, and I was off balance. So I started from the beginning. I listed everything I wanted to do for myself in a single day, starting with working out, the issue that exposed it all. Then I figured out how to make space for it in my day. Not easy when you're working twelve-hour days on set. But I had to find a way. Again, it was non-negotiable. The answer was in the morning. I began waking up one hour earlier to squeeze in a twenty-minute workout, a ten-minute meditation, and a bit of reading and writing.

At the other end of the day, the answer was to skip the 1:45 a.m. rum shot before the bar closed. I liked it, but I didn't need it. I rewired my priorities. And in the first few weeks, it felt awful. I was tired. Annoyed. I hated it. The bike rides were worse than ever. But soon, things started to shift. That extra hour in the morning became an hour and a half. Then two. Something was working.

Why? Because I implemented a foundational principle: organization. There's no secret formula here. While great things can sometimes emerge from chaos, without a clear structure, you will always find yourself lagging behind. Without organization, a real plan, a thoughtful routine, you have no compass. You are simply moving. And that's why it's critical to never confuse motion with action.

A rat in a cage can run at full speed on a wheel, that's motion. Running toward the finish line of a goal, that's action. Setting ourselves up for true action is incredibly difficult without a concrete plan. So, what does that mean, practically speaking? Let's break it down.

By now, you have a vision, something we established in Chapter One. But vision alone is never enough. You must translate it into tangible, actionable steps.

Let me give you a real example:

At our organization, we set out with a simple yet bold belief: screenplays deserve a place on every bookshelf. A beautiful idea, yes. But what's the action behind it? Here's what it looked like in practice:

- Identify six screenplays to publish by a specific date.

- Write forewords for each of them.

- Test the market and gather early feedback from potential readers.

- Research bookstores carrying similar works; identify key retailers.

- Craft a compelling pitch and prepare an irresistible presentation.

- Reach out to retailers and secure distribution commitments.

- Benchmark the best options for high-quality printing.

- Develop prototypes of the book.

- Launch a pre-order campaign to generate early traction.

- Release, distribute, and promote the final editions.

That's ten concrete steps, each one clear, measurable, and aligned with the end vision. There's no guesswork. No hoping. Just structured, purposeful action. I share this with you because we didn't just plan it, we lived it. And it worked.

On an even larger scale, look at the story of Tesla and the Cybertruck. They opened a waitlist years before the product was even available. That wasn't just marketing hype, it was a strategic action. They measured demand, generated massive anticipation, and simultaneously kept their broader plan in motion. The real enemy isn't failure, it's overthinking.

We waste extraordinary amounts of energy in hesitation, doubt, and second-guessing. When fear, stress, and anxiety creep in, rational thinking loses its place at the table. That's why planning is so powerful. It removes unnecessary decisions. It frees up your mental bandwidth. It gives you the clarity to focus on what truly matters.

And organization shouldn't exist only in your work, it must extend into your daily life.

You might feel like your personal life is chaotic. You might have demanding work hours, kids to take care of, or responsibilities piling up. It doesn't matter. Your reality is your reality. What matters is how you take control of it.

Here's a practical exercise:

- Take a pen and paper.

- Write down the days of the week.

- Start with the non-negotiables: work, family obligations, essential appointments.

- Look at the remaining gaps. That's your opening.

In those spaces, schedule two hours of deep, undistracted work. Protect that time like your life depends on it, because your dreams do. By doing this, you are no longer wishing for success, you are architecting it. You are building a roadmap where your daily reality serves your long-term vision. And soon, you'll face an unavoidable truth: not everything can fit.

This is where prioritization begins.

Ask yourself one powerful, clarifying question: What do I truly want to create? When you answer honestly, your priorities will arrange themselves. You have three kids? Beautiful. Give them all the time they deserve. I mean it, all the time they deserve. But that small window you find on Friday night? That's sacred. That belongs to your art, your calling, your future.

Maybe you love karaoke, and that's wonderful. But sometimes, you will have to say no. Because your purpose deserves your attention more than a fleeting night out. And here's something important:

Your true friends won't disappear just because you miss a few parties. In fact, many will respect you even more for honoring your path. And if they don't? Then perhaps they were never truly your friends to begin with.

## Mastering the Art of No: Protecting Your Time, Protecting Your Dream.

But here's the challenge: you have to learn to say no. Say it. Voice it. Own it.

- No, I can't do lunch today.
- No, I can't drive you to the airport.
- No, I don't have the bandwidth to help you with your Canva presentation.
- Hell no, I can't party on Friday, even though I would love to and love rum shots.

You're not a bad friend. You're not selfish. You're not becoming someone cold or self-centered. You're simply recognizing a truth that too many people ignore: You can't do it all.

I understand, you want to be there for everyone. I do too. But here's the danger: in trying to be everything for everyone, you risk losing yourself. You are the only constant in your life, the only person who will be with you from the very first breath to the very last. If you keep putting yourself last, how do you ever expect to move forward? How do you expect to bring your vision to life, to live your calling, to create the legacy only you can create?

Saying no is hard. It feels uncomfortable at first. But for your sake, for your future, it is one of the greatest skills you can master. I'm not saying that in a coachy way, but as a creator planning your time, saying no becomes your best weapon. And within that protected time, it's essential to create a space not for productivity, not for output, but for yourself.

A sacred moment. A reset.

What do you love to do? Walk in nature? Stargaze? Sit in silence, thinking about nothing at all? Whatever it is, schedule it, and guard it.

Honor it. Because this time isn't "wasted." It's vital. This is what renews you. This is what fills the well from which all creativity, all action, all strength will flow.

If seeing friends is part of your nourishment, that's wonderful, plan for it. But always with full awareness. Make sure your time remains aligned with your bigger picture. Living in constant urgency is not sustainable. Running breathless from one task to another is not living, it's surviving. And you deserve better than survival. You are here to thrive, to create, to build something meaningful.

That's why smart planning isn't about cramming your day with endless tasks. It's about moving with precision and intent.

Here's an important, no, mandatory, rule: do not overload your schedule.

You don't want your day to look like this:

- 9:00 a.m. — Meditation

- 9:25 a.m. — Go for a run

- 10:00 a.m. — Prospect calls (at least 3)

- 10:15 a.m. — Write 500 words

- 10:20 a.m. — Post an article on social media

That's not a plan. That's a recipe for burnout.

When you schedule like that, you don't own your day, your day owns you. And very quickly, you'll come to resent your own ambition. Your day must feel free. Spacious, and alive.

Three tasks, maximum, per day. Even fewer if you already have a full-time workload. And that's not a compromise, that's wisdom.

Step by step, you will go far.

## Putting in the Reps

The reality is simple, and brutal: no one is coming to save you. It's your job to be mindful of what you do, how you do it, and why you're doing it. Nobody will save you because nobody owes you anything. If you don't send that pitch for the brilliant series you have in mind, no one will magically knock on your door and say, "Hey beautiful stranger, by any chance, do you have a pitch for me?" It doesn't work that way. It never has, and it never will.

I used to be that person, the one pissed off at everything and everyone. I wanted everything: the results, the recognition, the life I dreamed of. But I wasn't putting in the reps. I was mediocre at everything because I wasn't dedicating enough time to anything. I was partying, eating out, wasting hours, and once back home, I would sit there, full of resentment, happily complaining about how unfair life was. "I'm great," I would tell myself. Great? Sure, buddy. I had potential, but no structure. Ambition, but no action.

One of my biggest problems at the time was the absence of a deep story. Not just working hard, but going deep. Immersing myself fully into something, body and soul. Creation only becomes transformative when you go deep, when you block out the noise, when you lose yourself in what truly matters. Your vision, that burning idea of who you want to become, won't appear while you're waiting idly by the door for someone to ring the bell. It emerges when you're deep into your craft, when you're too focused to even notice the door anymore. That level of dedication requires discipline. Not a rigid, joyless discipline designed to choke your life, but real, self-respecting discipline. The kind that starts with planning and evolves into commitment. It's not about locking yourself into misery. It's about making promises to your future self, and keeping them.

For some of you, even the word "discipline" might feel suffocating. If that's the case, fine. Then schedule freedom. Plan time to do nothing. Plan time to walk, to laugh, to breathe. Protect that breathing space like you would protect a rare treasure. Because without it, you'll suffocate your energy, and eventually, your passion too. If you create space for yourself to exist freely, you'll show up stronger when it's time to focus. Balance isn't a luxury, it's a strategy.

Still, let's be brutally honest: you can't do it all. There are sacrifices you'll have to accept along the way. And sacrifice isn't failure, it's clarity. You can't pile your plate sky-high and expect to move fast. Nor can you leave it empty and expect to be nourished. You need balance and to know exactly where you're aiming. With that vision in mind, you can organize your time with precision and remove the distractions that, for now, don't serve the bigger picture.

I'll give you a concrete example. I keep a list of everything I wish and want to do in my life. Right now, that list has over thirty items on it. Some of them are simple, like a sixty day hike in Japan. Others are bigger, like building a creative academy. They're all things I truly want to experience. But are they all urgent? Are they all aligned with my main mission today? No. So I don't abandon them, but I don't chase them either, at least not yet. I keep the list safe. I will revisit it. And when the time is right, I tackle each item one by one. They don't get lost. They don't get forgotten. They wait. And while they wait, I stay focused on what matters most right now. Otherwise, I will be the one to be forgotten.

It's a sacrifice, yes, but not a bitter one. It's a sacrifice made in harmony with myself. Because every step I take, every "no" I say today, is a "yes" to the bigger life I'm building. And believe me, the taste of that commitment is far sweeter than any temporary distraction ever could be. Don't fear the unknown, it's where all your victories are born.

There's one more thing I want to emphasize, something you should implement in your life starting right now. Shut up. The person who speaks first usually loses. A lot of power lives in the pause. You are wasting so much energy by commenting, debating, and having an opinion on everything. So shut up and get the reps in. As Steve Jobs said, focus your energy on the signal, not on the noise.

There is one exception, one crucial moment when speaking out loud becomes necessary: when you are manifesting what you are after. Declaring your goal aloud to someone you trust creates accountability. If you only whisper to yourself, "I'm going to write a book," that's nice, but it's also easy to let it slide. No one knows but you. But if, when the kids are finally asleep, you turn to your partner and say, "Hey love, I'm going to write a book", something shifts inside you. That spoken commitment pulls your dreams into the real world. And once it's out there, you don't want to be the person who only talks big and delivers nothing. My bet? The next morning, you'll sit down and start drafting your introduction. (It's what I did here)

So yes, talk to manifest. Other than that, shut up. Let your work speak louder than your words. Let your consistency build your story.

We've now explored the essential moves of a Creative Lifestyle. This list isn't complete, and it's not supposed to be. These are the fundamentals, the framework you must respect. Within these borders, you will write your own unique recipe. Your process will have its own nuances, its own adjustments. But if you follow the core principles laid out here, the entire game will start to shift in your favor.

You have now built the foundation of your creative lifestyle. Now it's time to go bigger. It's time to dive into the Creative Empire that will become the space you float in, the world you will build, rule, and expand.

# Chapter 3:

# Build a Creative Empire

We've discussed how setting yourself on the right path is essential. But alone, you can only go so far. You need to build a system around you that pulls you forward, that supports your growth, and that reminds you of who you are aiming to become. No matter how driven you are, if you walk alone for too long, you will eventually slow down. The right environment matters.

I can't emphasize enough the importance of learning from the best. This should be at the forefront of everything you take on. By reading and staying curious, you automatically position yourself ahead of most people. It's that simple, and that powerful. We are lucky to live in an era where we have near-infinite access to the knowledge of the brightest minds in history. Why not make the best of it? You can wake up and have a conversation with Marcus Aurelius. You can sip your coffee while absorbing Simone Weil's drive for justice and change. You can set your mind straight with Nelson Mandela's search for meaning or sharpen your logic with Daniel Kahneman's insights into human behavior. Everything is out there. There's no place to hide. And no excuse not to learn. If there's one thing I want you to remember in this chapter, in this whole book, it's the power of reading. Reading isn't supposed to be easy. It's like working out. Sometimes you're out of breath. Sometimes your muscles hurt. Sometimes you read an entire chapter and don't understand a thing. That's okay. That's part of the work. You're not broken, you're growing.

What matters is that you stay on the path. Read consistently. Surround yourself with the best ideas, the best thinkers, the best questions. Learn deeply. Let everything you absorb shape your own voice, your own style, your own empire. The more you engage with great minds, the more you step up to join their ranks. You will develop sharper thinking, a deeper understanding of human nature, and a stronger grasp of whatever field you choose to master.

So go for it. Dive in. Build your mind like an empire under construction, brick by brick, day after day.

Surrounding yourself with great thinkers is transformative. However, most of them have been dead for centuries, you can't exactly be friends with statues. That's where your core group comes in: the people you interact with daily. Your environment will either feed your ambition or slowly kill it. Choose wisely. Your core group will shape your actions, your standards, and ultimately, what you achieve.

**Choose Your Circle Wisely**

I had to leave a few friends behind, friends I had fun with, who meant something to me, but who couldn't help me grow, who couldn't hold me to a higher standard. At different stages of my life, I've found myself deeply influenced by the people around me. Sometimes, to a scary extent. After high school, I didn't really know what to do next. Film school wasn't on the table anymore. So I started working behind a bar in my hometown. At first, it felt fantastic. Parties every night. Flings. Inside jokes. I won my spot behind the counter, and all the tra-la-la. But deep down, I knew I didn't fit. So I adapted, without even realizing it. My coworkers weren't passing through. This was it for them. And that's fine, no judgment. But their rhythm became mine. Betting on horses before the shift started. Too many drinks. A little bag of white passed hand to hand. Late nights. Late meals. I wasn't being pulled into anything. I chose to follow. It's what everyone did, so I did it too. And honestly, most of them ended up owning their own bars or restaurants. They built something. That was their path.

But me? I started mimicking a lifestyle that wasn't mine. Wasting time, money, energy, on horses, on hangovers, on habits I didn't even believe in. It took me three years to snap out of it. Three years to stop, look back, and say: What the hell am I doing here? Then I ran.

And years later, in New York, I started dating a woman who had graduated from one of the top universities. Suddenly, I found myself surrounded by thinkers, builders, wealthy minds, creators, the kind of people I dreamed of becoming. And you know what? I wasn't pretending. I wasn't playing dress-up. I belonged. I started soaking it all in. Quietly, attentively. I was learning. And I knew I had changed circles. This time, on purpose.

You've probably heard this before: you are the average of the five people closest to you. Your mindset, your habits, even your income will reflect that circle. It's that simple, and that powerful.

If you spend your time with people who complain about the system, who find comfort in mediocrity, who let life happen to them without resistance, then inevitably, you will become one of them. Maybe not right away, but little by little, their inertia will seep into you. On the other hand, if you surround yourself with people who chase their dreams, who take action, who turn wild ideas into milestones, you will rise to meet them. Their energy will pull you upward.

I know this isn't always easy. Some of us live in places where the kind of energy we crave feels rare, or even nonexistent. But here's the good news: we live in a time where you can build your ecosystem online. You are no longer trapped by geography. Connect with thinkers on LinkedIn, X, or wherever they gather. Engage in real conversations. Don't network just to promote yourself. Seek relationships where value flows both ways, people who inspire you and people you can inspire in return.

You'd be surprised how many minds like yours are out there, waiting to be found. People who, just like you, are chasing something bigger than themselves. Surround yourself with them intentionally. Choose proximity to greatness, even if at first it's virtual. With time, it will become tangible.

Learning how to navigate people is a skill worth mastering. This is not about manipulation, it's about setting yourself up for success. It's about building an environment that challenges you to stay sharp, to think bigger, to move with conviction.

Who is teaching you? What are you learning? Who do you turn to when you hit a wall? If you don't have a mentor yet, start looking. There are people out there doing exactly what you want to do, and they carry insights that could save you years of wandering. Don't assume that all doors are closed. Don't assume you have to figure it all out alone. You'd be surprised how many people, busy, brilliant people, will take the time to answer a thoughtful, well-crafted email if you simply have the courage to ask. Try it. You have nothing to lose, and everything to gain.

## Seek Greatness, Take Responsibility

Of course, you probably won't get Oprah to offer you an internship tomorrow. But then again, why not try? Reach out to the creatives you admire, the ones who ignite something inside you. Ask a genuine, polite question. My bet? You'll get more answers than you expect. People who have walked the road before often recognize the hunger in others. They remember what it felt like to be where you are now.

These people can bring light to your journey. They can act as a compass, helping you navigate obstacles and stay aligned with your deeper mission. Feeling alone is one of the hardest parts of chasing creative greatness. It's easy to get discouraged, to feel directionless, to want to quit. But don't. You're not alone, even if sometimes it feels that way.

And if your dream mentor doesn't respond, that's okay. It doesn't mean you're not worthy. It just means you need to keep searching. Someone out there is willing to share wisdom, if you have the courage and humility to ask. And remember, seek out people who are smarter, more experienced, and more driven than you. Step outside your comfort zone. If you're always the smartest person in the room, you're already in the wrong room. Growth happens when you're challenged, not when you're comfortable.

If you're sitting there complaining that you don't know where to start, you've already fallen into the victim trap. Stop blaming the world for your situation. Own your truth. Own your next move.

I have kids at home, and one thing that drives me crazy is when they say, "Oh, it got broken." No, it didn't just "get broken." You dropped the plate. You broke the plate. Maybe it wasn't intentional, maybe it was an accident, but it was still you. Life works exactly the same way. Things don't just happen to you. You play a role, even when you don't want to admit it. If you want to move forward, take full responsibility for your failures and for your successes. Complaining keeps you stuck. Action moves you forward.

And this works both ways: own your mistakes, but also own your wins. Humility is crucial, but downplaying your achievements serves no one. Saying, "Yes, I built this," isn't arrogance, it's acknowledging reality. The way you frame your story matters. If you succeed, it's not luck. It's not because someone handed it to you. It's because you showed up when others didn't. You put in the reps when no one was watching.

If you keep hitting the same obstacles again and again, it's not your mom's fault. It's not your boss's fault. It's on you. Maybe you're not looking at the problem from enough angles. Maybe you're clinging to old solutions that no longer fit the size of your dreams.

How do you change that? By owning the full picture. By staying relentless. By asking better questions instead of recycling old excuses.

## Reset Your Mindset

Reset your mindset. Go back to the lifestyle principles from Chapter Two. Reread them if you must. Ground yourself again. And most importantly, start talking to yourself differently. That little pat on the back you've been waiting for from the world? Stop waiting. Give it to yourself. You deserve it. You've always deserved it.

Life, especially a creative life, is full of ups and downs. Everyone experiences them, but most people don't handle them well. They ride the highs like kings and crash through the lows like victims. But you must be different. Take Roger Federer, arguably the greatest tennis player of all time. He won only fifty four per cent of the points he played. And yet, he won eighty per cent of his matches. How? Because when he lost a point, he didn't dwell on it. He moved on to the next one. Instantly. No drama, no collapse, no loss of focus.

You lost a point? That's okay. Move on to the next one. Quickly, decisively, without letting it bleed into your future. And when you win? Acknowledge it, but don't let it define you. Do you really need to post it all over social media, scream about it, jump on the roof? Probably not. Because when your identity becomes tied to your victories, your joy becomes conditional, chained to the next win. And that's a dangerous, exhausting way to live.

A victory is not your identity. It's simply the natural outcome of a well-crafted strategy, of consistent reps, of deep alignment between vision and action. Look at the Oscars. Watch closely. The young winners often crumble under emotion, crying, losing their words, overwhelmed by the moment. Meanwhile, the veterans, the true masters, stay composed, almost serene. They've been here before. They understand: the award is an honor, yes, but it doesn't define them. It's not who they are.

If you let yourself be defined by the outcome, you will be miserable when the outcome doesn't come. Because success isn't automatic. It will happen, but ninety-nine per cent of your ideas, your projects, your dreams won't make the cut. Do you really want your happiness to depend on that one per cent?

Instead, anchor your fulfillment somewhere stronger. Let the work itself be your reward. Let the process, the craft, the discipline, the journey, be where your joy lives. Because that is the only place it will survive the long haul.

And in your creative empire, curiosity is a pillar you can't overlook. It keeps your mind fresh in an oversaturated world. There's immense power in curiosity. Resources are infinite. But in that infinity, you have to navigate wisely. You can't afford to lose yourself in distractions, jumping from one thing to the next without direction.

### The Power of Compound Interest

One lesson I learned late, but that changed everything, was compound interest. Growing up in a small town in the south of France, economy wasn't something people talked about much. Conversations were about football, horses, what to eat while we eat, and when to grab a coffee. The jobs were simple and respectable: lawyers, insurance brokers, restaurant owners, car dealers. Money wasn't a topic, it was almost taboo. I never really understood the concept of building wealth. I didn't even realize it was an option. Until reality hit me.

At some point, I realized: if I wanted to build a lifestyle that actually worked, I had to think long-term. I kept seeing the term "compound interest" everywhere but never really grasped it, until I did. And once you understand it, you start seeing it everywhere. Everything in life compounds. Your knowledge, your skills, your relationships. Every book you read, every experience you accumulate, every smart decision you make, it stacks on top of the last. Growth isn't linear. It's exponential. So don't fool yourself into expecting overnight change. Keep stacking. Tiny smart moves, done consistently, lead to transformations you can't even imagine yet.

I realized this with money too. (Quick disclaimer: I'm not a financial advisor. I'm just sharing what I've learned firsthand.) For a long time, I believed investing was only for a certain class of people, those with wealth, knowledge, access. That belief came from my environment, from the mindset of my hometown. We weren't educated about money. We still aren't.

One of my best childhood friends still says he can't invest because he doesn't have "enough" to start. I understand where that comes from, but it's wrong. I started with one hundred dollars. Adding fifty bucks here and there when I could. The habit mattered more than the amount. As a struggling artist, I was almost always broke, living paycheck to paycheck, when I even had a paycheck. But I still had one freedom no one could take from me: the choice of where to put the little money I had.

And here's what I learned: money disappears. If it sits in your pocket, or even in your bank account, it gets spent. It vanishes into rent, food, bills, small luxuries. Slowly, silently, almost invisibly. I didn't want to fight the system. I wanted to leverage it. So I started putting my money where it could grow. Even if it was just ten bucks at a time. I invested it. I set it. I left it alone. And I let it build. Small moves, repeated over time, changed everything.

If you're serious about building your creative empire, at some point, you'll have to take the leap and make your money work for you. Otherwise, you'll stay trapped in the cycle of always chasing the next paycheck, always dependent, always reactive. Financial freedom isn't about millions. It's not about luxury cars or mansions. It's about choice. It's about not wasting. It's about using the system to grow whatever you have, however small it may seem at the start.

To give you an idea: if you start with one hundred dollars at five per cent interest and add just another one hundred dollars per month for thirty years, you'll end up with about eighty thousand dollars. That's not a dream, it's simple math. Now, if your situation improves and you increase your monthly deposit by ten per cent each year, after thirty years, you'll have over three hundred twenty nine thousand dollars.

That's real. That's possible. That's available to almost anyone willing to commit and stay consistent.

I get that some people are in truly tough financial situations, where even saving a few dollars feels impossible. But if we're honest, most people can do this. The hard truth? We live in a materialistic society where we're constantly encouraged to spend without thinking. Most of us waste money on things we don't need, coffee runs, impulse buys, streaming subscriptions we forgot we had. The difference between long-term financial struggle and financial growth is often nothing more than a shift in habits.

Start small. Start now. You're not trying to win the lottery. You're trying to build something real, something that compounds silently, powerfully, until one day, you realize you gave yourself freedom.

## Build the Empire, Stay Hungry

It's a path opposite to the one of least resistance. But ask yourself, what are you seeking? Not every artist, creator, or writer has to struggle. This idea of the "starving artist" is a myth that too many people buy into. Sorry, but that's b***s***. Once you have your vision, even if you take a job to pay the bills, you can create a system that works for you. Put your plan into action. Don't waste energy looking at what others are doing. Keep your head up. Stay on your path.

As much as you want your business, your art, or your creative empire to grow, you have to balance growth with sustainability. That means tackling things one step at a time. There's no greatness in being scattered. If you try to do everything at once, you'll burn out before you build anything meaningful. But here's the key: whatever you're creating, whether it's a book, a business, a film, or a movement, make it an adventure. Because in the end, you're not just creating for yourself. You're building wealth, of mind and money. You're creating something that serves people, that brings value into homes. You're helping create jobs, opportunities, and inspiration. You're leaving a legacy. And that's what matters.

When you finally manage to create an ecosystem where you're surrounded by the best, the first thing you should do is act like you're not there yet. Why? Because it creates friction. And that friction keeps you reaching for more. The worst thing that could happen is for you to get comfortable. To think you've made it. Checked the boxes. Found your rhythm. No. That's when you fall asleep. That's when you lose. Remember this: this isn't an endless game. You're in a specific season of your life, one that demands full alignment. You are the architect of your empire, your life. You decide how it moves forward. Keep that vision in your mind at all times.

Allow yourself room to experiment. Don't be afraid to look bad. Don't be afraid to feel exposed. When you're building something new, only you see the whole vision. Others won't get it, and that's fine. What you must never lose is your integrity with yourself. Every time you feel tempted to slack off, stop, or lower the volume, remember who you are. You're someone who keeps their word, especially to themselves. At home, at work, in your studio, wherever you show up. Write it down if you need to. It's as powerful as a standing ovation. You're reinforcing your identity, one action at a time.

It takes crazy courage to dive into deep introspection, to challenge your beliefs, to confront your own patterns. We're wired to lie to ourselves. Knowing that, act for your own good. Build the framework that sets you up for real, long-term success. In your empire, gold seeding is key. Not as some Excel sheet checklist, but as a long-term vision. What do you want to conquer? What actually excites you? Be bold and optimistic when setting your gold seeds, because they'll become your companions, always there, walking with you,

lighting the path toward whatever you're here
to create.

We've been dragged into pessimistic territory,
war, climate collapse, right-wing extremists,
left-wing extremists, terrorism. Fear
everywhere. The end is near. We're all doomed.
But I don't buy it. All this darkness is thrown
in your face because drama sells. If news
channels started telling you the world was
getting better, you know what would actually
start getting worse? Their ratings. They have to
show you the helicopter crash, the tragedy, the
violence. That's the playbook. The media is
standardized enough to take something rare
and turn it into a general feeling, no doubt.

But look realistically at what's in front of you.
Be an optimist. Be a realist. Be conscious of
what's happening and of all the good you can
still create. That's the mindset. And your
mindset is the empire.

Now, let's explore the power of storytelling,
how the world is wired today, and how to take

advantage of it by understanding how it works.

# Chapter 4:

# The Storytelling Influence

Everyone over twenty-five has a memory of an ad that stuck. Something that anchored itself in your mind, not because you bought the product, but because it hit something deeper. For me, it was a Royal Canin, a dog food commercial: thirty seconds of slow motion, dogs running free to the rhythm of "She May" by Ennio Morricone. Pure magic. I watched it on loop. I couldn't believe how good it was. How cinematic. How emotional. How memorable.

And what about "Think Different" when Apple reinvented the game. "They push the human race", I remember hearing that line and thinking how amazing it was for a brand to embody such a powerful message.

Unfortunately, those kinds of ads are now a relic. Not because they weren't brilliant, they were. But because storytelling has changed. The playing field is different. Attention is fragmented. Context has shifted. We don't watch content the way we used to. Today, what works doesn't work the same way.

A single beautiful piece of content is no longer enough. The internet doesn't have time for slow-motion poetry. We've entered the era of quantity and quality. Brands, creators, artists, we all need to show up with volume and precision. Not just to be liked, but to even be noticed. You're not just competing with others in your field. You're competing with everything. With an infinite scroll of dopamine, distractions, and chaos. With cats falling off shelves. With breaking news, trending dances, babies, memes, tragedies, TikToks. The new baseline is noise.

Look at a beautiful advertisement that didn't move the needle: Montblanc, in 2024, decided to reappropriate its story. Tired, perhaps, of being associated with boring, fifty-something white men, they partnered with none other than Wes Anderson. Montblanc and Wes Anderson in the same sentence already feels like a stretch, but they did it.

And the result? It was mesmerizing.

I genuinely loved what they created. The problem is: I was probably one of the few who watched it all the way through. From what insiders say, the campaign didn't deliver the impact they expected. They went all in, and they went wrong. Not with the story itself, but with the approach. How unfair is the world today, even for creators who try to do something beautiful?

So how do we cut through?

We go deeper. The surface story is no longer enough. That dog with Morricone? Today, it would get a like. Maybe a share. Then disappear. If you want to last, you have to mean something. You have to reach past logic and hit emotion. Storytelling has evolved into something multidimensional, a dance between psychology, identity, values, rhythm, and resonance.

We don't just need to tell stories anymore. We need to embody them. Live them. Build worlds around them. In this new landscape, your story isn't just a pitch, it's your DNA. And once you learn how to code that DNA into your message, you stop chasing the algorithm. The algorithm starts recognizing you.

We may resist the word brand. It can feel like a betrayal to artists, a word from the world of marketing that doesn't belong in the studio. But that's an illusion. Being a brand today doesn't mean being a sellout. It means being intentional. It means showing up with clarity. Like it or not, you are your own brand. Your name, your work, your message, that is the brand. And if you don't define it, others will define it for you.

Look around. The CEO used to be a ghost, someone who popped up once a quarter for an earnings call, shook a few hands, then vanished behind a boardroom. Now? They're on podcasts. Weekly. They're tweeting. They're sharing their bookshelf, their mindset, their morning routine. They're letting people in.

That's not a trend. It's a paradigm shift. Social media didn't just connect us, it rewired the system. We no longer trust entities. We trust people. We want to see who's behind the curtain. That's why the perfectly filtered, overly polished images barely register anymore. They look good, yes, but they feel empty. They don't move us.

## Show Up or Fade Out

What moves us now is realness. Someone looking us in the eye and telling the truth. Someone showing up without the mask. That's what creates engagement, not in a manipulative way, but in a human way. We've entered an era where sincerity is the most disruptive force you can embody.

We're coming out of a collective crisis of consciousness, one that still lingers beneath the surface. We've been alienated from ourselves, from each other, from the insane pace of this world. We're desperate for something that feels true again. And that's where the artist steps in. Not with answers. But with presence. With voice.

When Taylor Swift speaks, millions feel like she's talking directly to them. That's not luck, and it's not just fame. It's intentional storytelling. She built a brand that feels personal, intimate, human. And that's the key. We all want to feel special. That's the whole game. That's the network.

So when you show up as yourself, raw, intentional, and clear, you're not "branding" in the corporate sense. You're creating a mirror for someone else to see themselves in. That's the power of art. And that's the storytelling influence.

Many of us born in the late 80s, I'm 1989, still say things like "I don't want to be seen" or "I'm not comfortable on camera." I get it. I really do. That narrative protected us for years. It lets us stay humble. Stay hidden. But that framework is done. The rules have changed. Visibility isn't optional anymore. It's part of the job. We've spent years talking about "influencers," a word that comes to mean everything and nothing. But here's the truth:

you want to be one. Not in the shallow, Instagram-filtered, mass-market sense, but in the most intentional, value-driven way possible. You want to influence people toward what you care about. You want to move your niche. You want to create impact by being deeply, unapologetically you.

We'll dive deeper into audience-building soon. But before that, this shift has to be acknowledged. Because the world moved. And if you don't move with it, you don't become mysterious, you become invisible. Scrolled past. Forgotten.

The real game now is perception. You are influencing how someone sees you, sure. But more importantly, you're influencing how they see themselves after encountering you. That's power. That's resonance. And if we're honest, influence is a relationship. Think of a couple: two people, two perspectives, two inner worlds. What makes it work is the ability to see the other person's world, and invite them into yours. That's connection. And we are still wired for that, even in a hyper-digital world. Even with ten tabs open, a screen in our palm, and a swarm of distractions. That hunger for connection hasn't faded. It's grown stronger.

So no, this isn't about being a perfect speaker or flawless on camera. This is about showing up. Not for attention, but for alignment. So that the person who needs your voice, your story, your presence can actually find it.

You don't need to perform. You just need to be there. Because presence is what cuts through the noise. You want attention? You either command it, or stick in someone's mind long enough to matter. What you're aiming for is a presence that becomes conscious in someone else's world.

Everyone is trying to leverage this new digital era. But you? You'll be a step ahead. Because by deeply connecting, you're not just creating content. You're generating emotion. And emotion is psychological. It doesn't fade. It stays. It shapes people. And that's the highest form of storytelling.

## Emotion Is the Engine

Love is a secret weapon. You can live without it, sure. But let's be honest: we're all thirsty for it. It fuels us, shapes us, defines what we seek and what we avoid. When I hear people say young folks today are just robots behind screens, I can't help but shake my head. Who said they don't feel anything? Who said they don't understand? That's the old world speaking. They understand deeply, they're just wired differently.

We've never been this close to our emotions. Never been this exposed to ourselves. When I grew up, a boy couldn't cry, that was something girls did. Now we talk about vulnerability in podcasts, in songs, in everyday conversations. Girls don't just fall for the loudest guy in the room anymore. They fall for the one reading quietly on a bench. Books are sexy. We share our therapist's number like it's a favorite café. We try EMDR. We meditate. We journal. We slow down. Our well-being, for the first time, has become a priority.

The storytelling shifted, and with it, the doors to another realm opened. Emotions are now the road to connection. And if you want to tell a story that's genuinely yours, this step isn't optional. It's mandatory. You can't bypass the heart and expect people to follow.

Noise is everywhere. But the most powerful messages don't tell you what to think, they shift how you feel. They hit you in the gut. They don't shout. They resonate. That's the new blueprint. Brevity with depth. Every second counts. Cut the fluff. Keep the punch. Emotional logic. People don't remember facts, they remember how you made them feel. Immersive narratives. Whether it's a film, a brand, a conversation or your own journey, the key isn't to talk about the moment. It's to pull people into it. Because if your message doesn't move people, it's just more noise adding to the mess.

## Own Your Voice, Own Your World

Our generation discovered the power of ownership, not through brands, but by becoming one. We stopped renting out our time and started owning our vision. It's not about clocking hours anymore. It's about building something that lasts.

We've talked about creativity. We've talked about building your empire. And this is what the new wave of talent gets instinctively: everything around you: your work, your story, your value is within your control. That doesn't mean over-controlling. It means owning what's yours so you can grow it, protect it, and monetize it, your way.

Before I created Artist Lab, I was always amazed, and honestly, appalled, by how the system worked. Publishing companies taking eighty per cent of a photographer's earnings. Record labels squeezing the life out of musicians. As a screenwriter, I watched the same few people line their pockets while the rest struggled. My cousin, a successful street artist, sold his paintings for $5,000 but walked away with $1,000. And that was considered good. For me, that had to stop.

The artist is the center. Not a cash cow to be squeezed dry by middlemen. Everyone within the framework should be working for the artist, paid, of course, but not exploiting. The same goes for entrepreneurs. You come in with a great idea, no certainty you'll even survive the year, and if you do, good luck lasting three. Because everyone out there is planning to extract from you. Marketing "gurus", Website "designers.", and my favorite, the logo guy who calls himself a "studio" and charges a fortune.

When you start, all you have is your story. You build around it. And in this new world, you have to be the one who crafts your storytelling influence. Everything else is noise. Yes, you'll need to organize things. You'll need help. But one step at a time. What matters most: keep ownership.

Your life becomes a creator-led brand. You are your own media company. Barriers are down. You're both a brand and the master of your craft.

The storytelling influence isn't about getting views. It's about building something that lasts. It's the art of creating an audience that doesn't just click, but stays. One that engages because they feel seen. Because your story isn't just yours anymore, it becomes theirs. You do this through honesty. Through behind-the-scenes glimpses. Through truths they weren't expecting to hear but needed to. The kind that hit home, quietly and powerfully.

"How do you build that audience? Where do you find them?". That's the wrong question. It's not about finding. It's about attracting. Storytelling has changed, and with it, the entire way we think about attention. You don't chase an audience. You become someone worth following. You become a signal in the noise. In this dynamic, yes, the audience is king. But you are the queen. And one doesn't exist without the other. The game is collaborative now. All the cards are on the table.

Here's the first mental reset: you don't need a massive audience. We all see what happens with hundreds of thousands, even millions of followers. Good for them. But that's not what you're after. You don't need a crowd, what you need is a community. You need your niche. The right people. The ones who resonate. The ones who would pay, share, comment, and show up because it matters to them. Your mission isn't to go viral, it's to go deep. And to do that, you have to understand how your people think. What they care about. What makes them act. What stories they're waiting for someone like you to tell.

If you spend your energy polishing a perfect feed but never take the time to look at the human being behind the screen, no one will care. No one will buy it. No one will believe it. Without an audience, you're the CEO of nothing. A charming assassin with no one to aim at. Because the audience is always on the other end of the call, and you're rarely on the line alone. Speak to them with the right tone. With the right words. Not from a pedestal, but from within their world. When you get that right, you unlock something most people spend years chasing: trust. And once you have trust, the rest follows.

The strategy to create authentic, lasting art is personal. It can't be copy-pasted. It belongs to you, designed for the silent judges, the invisible eyes, the people you may never meet but who feel what you do. Your role is to make your truth ready for the world. And here's the beautiful twist: your audience won't just be spectators. If you build the relationship the right way, they'll become your collaborators.

You start to see what they respond to. What they love. What they share. And suddenly, you're not alone anymore. You're surrounded by people who get it. Who want in. Who feel part of something bigger than themselves. That's when it stops being just an audience, and starts becoming a movement.

You're not just building a fanbase. You're building an army. Not in the military sense, but in the strategic sense. You're a general with a vision, gathering the right people around a cause, a vibe, a pulse. You don't need fame. You need alignment. You need purpose. And with that, you can impact ten thousand people more deeply than a rural politician impacts their town. Real influence doesn't look like a follower count. It looks like a transformation.

And once your message hits, something incredible happens: you stop chasing people. They come to you. They become your ambassadors, your unofficial sales agents, your front line. That's why you treat them with care. You show respect. You don't copy/paste generic captions. You write with intention. Because it matters. Even if AI could save you three hours, your hand-crafted message has weight. It may not win on structure or syntax, but it wins on soul.

Machines can fake style. They can't fake the truth (yet?). And your audience can tell. They can feel when they've been seen. They can smell when it's real. If you disrespect their intelligence, their time, their attention, your message will fall flat. And soon, you'll be the one complaining that "no one gets what I'm trying to do." But when they engage, I mean really engage, it's magic. Because in a world where everything feels fake, realness is rare. And rare is valuable. They're not just giving you a like. They're giving you time. Curiosity. Trust. They're opening a door. Letting you inside. They're challenging your ideas, questioning your intent, cheering for your wins. How powerful is that? And they're doing it for you. Never forget it. And at the same time, never let them dictate your creative process. This relationship is about respect, not submission.

Start by observing. Zoom into your niche. Don't just write " I play music" or "I create art." Write what you really are in "Afro-futuristic drum beats with Portuguese ceramic textures." That's a niche. That's a signal. That's precise enough to attract, and repel. You don't want everyone. You want the right ones. Test the market. See how people react. The big players throw ten thousand dollars at Facebook Ads and read the analytics. You don't have that? Doesn't matter. You have curiosity. Use the free tools. Instagram tells you how many posts use a word. Explore. Type things in. See what communities gather around what you love. Ask yourself: why does their audience show up? What's the real magnet?

And if you're selling skincare, ask yourself, who are you in the ad? The mom playing peekaboo in soft lighting? Or the founder, bold and direct, explaining how the product works? There's no right answer. But there is a true one. And your job is to own it. Sometimes, the most powerful thing you can do is just point the camera at what's real, and let the story tell itself.

You need to get in your audience's head. Not to manipulate, but to understand. You're not trying to sell. You're trying to respond. To mirror a problem. To offer something that fills a quiet void. Something they didn't even realize they were looking for. When you speak, don't position yourself as the savior. You're not here to teach a lesson or fix their lives. You're just here to remind them of something they already know. You're here to show them where to look. That's it. Be a flashlight, not a sermon. No one wants to be told what to do. Even when your content is good, it won't land if it comes with moral superiority.

Remember: your audience is already overstimulated. They scroll through more in one hour than previous generations consumed in a week. You don't have fifteen minutes. You have twenty seconds, maybe thirty, to deliver a full-length emotional movie. Do I think it's possible? Not only do I think it's possible, I think it's essential. Because today's attention economy rewards only one thing: emotional, personal storytelling with a touch of tension.

And at the core of all of this is conflict. The gap between where they are and where they want to be. The emotion behind the choice. The tension before the transformation. That's where stories live. That's where your message sticks.

## Storytelling Is Strategy

Conflict is what keeps people on the edge of their seats. It's the cliffhanger. The contradiction. The unexpected twist. It's the tension between what is and what could be, and it's what keeps us watching, listening and reading. That's why storytelling techniques are no longer optional. They're not just creative tools. They're psychological strategies. And they are mandatory if you want to influence anyone, in any medium.

The good news? You can learn them. We all can. That's the one arena where we're all equal. The techniques exist. The blueprints are there. The only difference is whether or not you believe they'll work for you. If you believe you're capable of using them. If you're willing to apply them with clarity, discipline, and heart.

You've seen the offers. We all have.
"seventy-nine per cent discount! Limited time only!"
"Save your spot. Seven hours, thirty-eight minutes, fourteen seconds left."
"Only two copies left."
"The book that will change your life."
"Limited fine print edition."
"Only one left."
"Ninety per cent off."
You know the drill.

That's what I call psychological cloud influence. They're not selling, they're scripting. They're crafting messages to trigger your brain before your logic can catch up. They're pulling emotional levers to push you toward action. It's not about information, it's about urgency, scarcity, status, loss aversion. They don't talk to the rational you. They talk to the primal you.

But here's the truth: if you're trained, if you know what you're looking at, you won't fall for it. Why? Because it's not personal. It's engineered. And your brain knows the difference. That doesn't mean those techniques are wrong. It means they only work if they're used in alignment with authenticity.

Your authentic self, armed with these tools, now that gets attention. Real attention. The kind that lasts. The kind that moves people. The kind that resonates in any context, any culture, any language. Because people don't respond to tactics alone. They respond to truth wrapped in technique.

Robert Cialdini, in his book Influence, outlines the psychological levers that govern human behavior. One of the most powerful is reciprocity, the simple truth that when someone gives us something of value, we instinctively want to give something back. It's deeply wired. And it applies to your audience. If you give value first, whether that's insight, emotion, knowledge, perspective, your audience feels seen, respected, and engaged.

They want to stay. They want to go deeper. You gave first.

Take Pixar. They know this better than anyone. In the first five minutes, they'll hit you with a deep emotional punch. And because you're cracked open, they can then bring the twist later, and it lands. You're receptive. You've already surrendered. That's not manipulation. That's mastery. There's a difference.

Now let's be honest: most online creators use these strategies poorly. You've seen the low-effort booklets. The "free risk assessments." The "no cost, no catch" checklists. It's the bait, and you can smell the trap from a kilometer away. At least I can. And even if people fall for it, they rarely stay. Because what hooked them wasn't real value. It was fear of missing out. That doesn't build a relationship. That builds a transaction.

Take the classic: "fifty per cent off your first order." It works. That's psychology at play. But does it create loyalty? Will it retain the client? Will it build trust? Probably not. Because there's no connection. And if there's no connection, there's no long-term growth. What you want is not a sale, it's a relationship. What you want is resonance.

That's why I write twice a week on LinkedIn. Not to sell something fast. Not to get clicks or dopamine hits. I write because I care about the people on the other side. I care about the long game. I care about what we're building together. And people feel that. When it's real, they know.

## The Power of Commitment

Then there's the desire to keep your audience committed. And consistent. In a world where everything is competing for their attention, that's not easy. There's so much noise. So many distractions. So many reasons to scroll away. But one thing hasn't changed: if you hook them early, they'll stay. You don't need to give everything up front. Even something small, a spark, a question, a glimpse, can be enough to earn their attention for the long haul.

TV shows do this all the time. They open the pilot with a flash-forward, a dramatic moment pulled from the end of the season. It doesn't resolve anything, but it creates tension. It opens a loop. That's a new kind of storytelling: one that builds early commitment. Now yes, it can become mechanical if used like a gimmick. But when used with care, with real narrative weight, it builds trust. And trust leads to connection.

Then there's the best-selling book effect. People trust what other people trust. It's pure psychology. You want to book a trip? You check the Airbnb reviews. You want to buy a product? You scroll through the Amazon ratings. We live in a world of stars, comments, and testimonials. So use that. Show proof. Highlight real feedback. Let your audience know they're not alone, that others have walked this road before them. It gives them confidence. It gives you credibility.

But above all: be honest. Don't fake the numbers. Don't invent reviews. Don't manufacture testimonials. Audiences today are sharper than ever. They've seen it all. They can spot something off in two seconds flat, like a product with three thousand five hundred and ninety-three glowing reviews… two days after launch. Or twenty-five testimonials that all sound like they were written by the same intern on Google Maps. They know. And when they feel lied to, they don't forgive.

So don't lie. Don't try to cheat your way into trust while pretending to apply good strategy. The real strategy is this: use your tools, but use them well. Thoughtfully. Authentically. Everything we've talked about, conflict, scarcity, emotion, tension works. But it only works long-term if it's real.

We've already talked about scarcity. It's one of the strongest motivators we have. When something is rare, we want it. When something is about to disappear, we lean in. FOMO is not just a trend, it's hardwired into us. So yes, use it. But don't fall into the trap of false urgency. Cheap countdown timers, fake "only two left" warnings, artificial waitlists, these things might work once, but they destroy long-term trust.

Instead, offer something truly scarce. Something real. Something that can't be faked. Like a behind-the-scenes moment with you. Like direct access to your creative process. Like something personal and unfiltered. That's rare. That's powerful. That's meaningful.

Whatever strategy you choose, always remember this: your audience is not a target. They're partners. Allies and humans. The moment you lose respect for them, you lose everything. So build with them. Grow with them. Move up the ladder together. Because the best audiences aren't bought, they're built. And once they trust you, they don't just follow. They stay.

# Chapter 5:

# The Creative Playbook

There are no shortcuts. No secret trapdoors.
No formula whispered only to the lucky few.
There are just tools, strategy, and the grind.
You've done the inner shift, your mindset has
evolved. You've started to see yourself as a
brand. But now, it's time to take the next step:
to think like a strategist.

A creator doesn't just produce things. A creator
builds a system. A machine. A personal
infrastructure that keeps producing, even
when you're not in the mood, even when
you're juggling five things, even when the
pressure is high. This is where the creative
playbook comes in: not as a rigid rulebook, but
as a dynamic framework you can return to. A
living document of how you operate at your
best.

One of the first key principles of this playbook
is diversification. You're not here to bet
everything on one card. You're not building a
delicate tower that crumbles the second one
piece fails. You're building something stronger.
Smarter. A resilient creative portfolio. Look

around, filmmakers don't pitch one film. They pitch a slate. Painters don't hang a single canvas. They curate collections. Fashion brands don't drop one piece, they launch lines. So why would you, as a writer, a founder, an artist, a thinker, only allow yourself one shot?

Even if you're working on one major project, a book, a film, a startup, you can still build an ecosystem around it. You can write short essays. Share behind-the-scenes thoughts. Create a newsletter. Document your process in mini-docs. Tell stories from the side angles. Make it layered. Make it alive. One masterpiece equals many access points.

And yes, you can manage multiple projects. The secret? They don't all have to move at the same speed. That's the parallel project method. It's not about juggling everything at once. It's about placing each idea on its own timeline. One project might be deep in production. Another is marinating in development. A third lives in your notes app, not yet born, but breathing. That's what your roadmap is for.

That project you've almost finished? Line up the release. That one you shelved six months ago? Reopen the file, see what's still alive. That idea you've been daydreaming about but never dared to write down? Start giving it shape. Let it breathe. Give it a name. Write a single sentence. Let it stretch.

Because when you lay it all out, you realize something powerful: there is room. You don't have to kill one dream to make space for the next. With the right system, you can nurture multiple lanes. Your pace becomes sustainable. Your vision becomes clear. Your creativity becomes intentional.

The opposite of that? Chaos. Creative burnout. Projects scattered and half-built. Ideas that fade because you never gave them structure. That's what happens when we operate without a playbook. And it drags the whole machine backward, your energy, your self-trust, and your growth.

You can't afford that. You need stimulation. New brain food. New sparks. If you don't feed your mind, it starts feeding on itself. That's how burnout starts: not from overwork, but from creative starvation.

This chapter is about building the system that protects your energy and multiplies your impact. This is the blueprint. This is the creative playbook.

Let's build it.

### Think in Leverage. Act with Vision.

When you create, don't just think about the piece of work in front of you. Think about how to expand it, how to leverage what you're already doing with minimum additional effort and maximum impact. That might sound counterintuitive, especially if, like most of us, you were raised to value hard work above all. Push harder. Go further. Out-hustle everyone. But the creative path isn't always about working harder.

Leverage is about recognizing what's already in your hands, and building from it. It means asking: What's the next layer of this? Where else can it live? How can this idea breathe in another format? Take a book. That book can become a screenplay. That screenplay can turn into a film. The film can give birth to a TED Talk. That talk can become a course. That course can become a movement. One seed, many branches.

Look at George Lucas. He didn't just create Star Wars. He retained the rights to everything around it, characters, merchandise, future content. That's the real story. He didn't just build a franchise. He built a world. A brand. A legacy. And the leverage was always in his hands. At your scale, do the same. You don't need a studio. You need intention. Always think three-dimensionally. One piece of content can open five new doors, if you're bold enough to look.

That said, having a clear creative path isn't always easy. Distractions are everywhere. That's why I use what I call the Big Bet Rule, a twist on the classic Pareto Principle. You know the 80/20 rule: Eighty per cent of your time should go toward high-impact, high-value work. The kind that pays the bills. Builds the brand. Pushes the vision forward. That's your main game. Your foundation.

But the other twenty per cent? That's your playground. That's where you bet big. That's where you allow risk, chaos, curiosity. That's where you say, "Why not?" and go build something weird, spontaneous, unexpected. It might flop, but it might also be the thing that changes your trajectory entirely. It's a small percentage of your time, but it holds massive potential. Sometimes, all that holds us back is hesitation, that slow breath of doubt before we act. You know the one. Stretch beyond it.

Apply the ten-year lens. Don't just focus on today's metrics. Zoom out. Think about the version of yourself you're building over the next decade. Because here's the truth: you're already on the path to greatness. In ten years, you will arrive exactly where you've aimed, consciously or not. So give your future self a fighting chance. Make decisions that serve the long game. Maybe today you're buying a tiny apartment. Doesn't matter. You're playing for the house. The one with the view. The one with the studio. The one with space to breathe.

Plan accordingly, not for now, but for who you're becoming.

And when I say I know you'll get there, I'm not selling fantasies. I'm not making false projections. I'm telling you this: when you do the work, when you show up with clarity and consistency, you will arrive. Maybe you won't be Zuckerberg or Mark Cuban. So what? You're not trying to become them. You're becoming you. And that's entirely within reach.

We all have this beautiful opportunity:
To see it.
To believe it.
To build it.

## Momentum Over Perfection

Think long term. Always. But when it comes to execution, give momentum the upper hand. Momentum beats perfection every single time. Why? Because perfection is a seductive trap. It feels noble, but it kills creative businesses. Perfection delays decisions. It breeds hesitation. It slows your growth under the false pretense of quality control.

Here's the truth: you can always refine later. Polish comes with time. But if you don't release, you might never get anything out at all. There will always be something, a reason, an excuse, a subtle form of fear dressed up as professionalism, that convinces you to hold back. Like that actor who refuses to watch himself on screen because he "doesn't like how he looks." Good thing he's not the one in charge of releasing the movie. The same goes for you. Your personal discomfort cannot be the gatekeeper of your creative impact.

Instead of aiming for flawless, aim for the One Hundred Iteration Rule. Put this into your system: you're not allowed to judge your project until you've done it one hundred times. One hundred posts, one hundred pages, one hundred reps. That's your threshold. Not to prove anything to others, but to give yourself room to evolve. Iterations aren't just for testing ideas, they're for discovering what your work becomes when you let it breathe in the real world.

Too often, I see creatives collapse after one piece of feedback. One negative comment. One lukewarm reaction. And suddenly, the whole vision is in doubt. That's not sustainable. That's not how professionals operate. You need to release, then detach. Step back. Let the world react without it breaking you. Let the dust settle. Then observe. Analyze. Learn, and grow. If you don't do this, you'll live in a constant reactive loop, adjusting too early, tweaking too often, and never truly committing to forward action.

Let's talk about productivity. That word triggers people. For some, it's motivational. For others, it feels like pressure, like a corporate buzzword that doesn't belong in creative life. Same with "systems." Sounds cold. Sounds robotic. But for me, productivity has nothing to do with color-coded apps or sticker-covered planners. I don't care how pretty your calendar looks.

Real productivity is this: the deals you make with yourself. The inner contract. The one that says: "This matters, and I'm showing up for it." Productivity is knowing what needs to be done, knowing what you already have, and setting clear boundaries to protect the time and energy to make it happen.

If you can hold yourself to that, even imperfectly, you'll already be ahead of ninety per cent of people. Not because you're faster. Not because you're smarter. But because you've decided. You've chosen structure over chaos. And structure creates space. Space creates clarity. Clarity unlocks movement.

And movement? That's how things get built.

## The Power of the Daily Sprint

One of the most powerful boundaries you can create for yourself? The non-negotiable daily sprint. A fixed window of time. Every day. Dedicated to creation. No excuses. No multitasking. No notifications. No "just five minutes" on Instagram. Just you and your work.

On paper, it sounds simple. But in practice? It's hard. It's really hard. Some days, it's frustrating. Some days, it's excruciating. Because while you sit there trying to focus, the rest of the world is speeding through your mind. Messages. Responsibilities. Doubts. The sprint isn't just about what you create, it's about what you overcome to stay in it.

And yet, it's mandatory. You don't show up "when you feel like it." You don't wait for the perfect emotional weather. You show up regardless. This is not passive. This is not vague. This is not "let's see how I feel today." This is sacred.

Once you establish this rule, truly commit to it, you begin to take real ownership of your creative output. It becomes a rhythm. The repetition breeds confidence. The resistance loses its power. And slowly, you start to trust yourself. You don't just say you're a creator. You start to feel like one. Because you're doing the work. Every day. No performance, no pretending. Just you and the thing you love.

This daily sprint becomes your anchor. Your ritual. Your proof. That no matter what happens around you, there's a part of your day that's yours. Untouchable and protected.

I know how demanding this is. I know how strong the resistance can feel, the fatigue, the overthinking, the tiny whispers of "maybe later." But if you give in to that, you give your power away. Do not let yourself off the hook. Not this time. Not again..

## Zero Friction, Full Flow

If you're serious about showing up daily, you need to create a zero-friction setup. I can't stress this enough. For years, I underestimated how much small obstacles drain creative energy. A cluttered space. A pinging phone. An "urgent" email. It doesn't take much to break your rhythm. And when your rhythm breaks, your momentum goes with it.

Be honest with yourself. If you're writing but checking Instagram every ten minutes, you're not writing, you're pretending to. And again, no judgment. We're wired for distraction. But that's exactly why you need to act proactively. Don't wait to get better at resisting. Remove the trigger. Cut the loop before it starts.

Start with your phone. Your inbox. Notifications. Tabs. Noise. All of it needs to go. You don't need more willpower, you need better systems. Make your creative space so frictionless that the only thing left to do is create. And make it enjoyable. Turn it into a ritual if that helps. Light a candle. Close the door. Put on noise-cancelling headphones. Set a timer. Make the environment work for you. Because here's the thing: the fewer excuses you leave lying around, the faster you hit flow. And flow is the state where real work happens. Not reactive work. Not scattered productivity. Real, focused, original output. And to get there, you need to remove decisions. That's where automation comes in.

Let's be honest, we live in a golden era. Tools, processes, AI, everything is here. Right now. High-powered, affordable, accessible technology. Use it, and build your systems with it. Automation isn't just for startups and coders. It's your creative ally. It saves time, and that time? You reinvest it where it matters most.

Start small. Your email, your calendar, start by automating what repeats. You can set reminders, build templates, sync your meetings. These tools are your personal assistant, if you let them be. At home, same rule. Don't spend two hours figuring out what to cook. Pick five meals every Monday, make the list once, and move on. Every decision you pre-make is one less drain on your mental bandwidth.

And yes, AI is a game changer. We're only scratching the surface. I use it for transcripts. For structure. For clarity. It saves me hours every week. Use it intentionally. Let it support your focus. Not replace you, but free you. Even your phone can help you now. With screen time limits, app blockers, deep work modes. Use everything that supports your craft. Because all of it is part of your creative system.

Zero friction. That's the rule. Not to be rigid. But to be ready.

### Thematic Workdays & Whole-System Focus

We've talked about the parallel project method, that ability to manage multiple creative paths at once by placing them at different stages. But there's another powerful element in planning that keeps your brain sharp and your progress consistent: batching and setting thematic workdays.

This isn't about productivity hacks. It's about mental clarity. You can't be in deep ideation mode while also managing emails, hopping on Zoom calls, and writing three pages of copy. Your mind gets diluted. You lose the thread. That's why separating idea days from execution days is so important. You want your brain to hold one idea at a time, and go deep. Not skim the surface of ten things at once.

Design your week accordingly. Have dedicated creation days. Days for pure ideation and concept work. Other days for execution and editing. And some for connection, outreach, collaboration, visibility. That's the full picture. Because this isn't just about making things. It's about maintaining momentum. And momentum comes from rhythm.

That doesn't mean locking yourself away day and night, torturing yourself to find your next big idea. It means immersive sessions, intentional deep dives into your craft, balanced with time to breathe, connect, and build traction. The real creative process isn't just isolated genius. It's a whole ecosystem that includes both silence and signal.

Personally, I like to plan my week every Sunday. I sit down, take a moment, and map it out. That gives me clarity. I know where my attention is going. I can schedule my daily sprint around it. And I can batch work by theme, one day for creation, one day for strategy, one day for outreach. It's simple, but powerful.

The key is this: no more than two or three goals per week. And to be honest, for most people? Two goals is the sweet spot. It keeps the pressure off. It gives you room to breathe. It gives your creative mind the space it needs to exist, without feeling like it's drowning under a to-do list.

**Reverse the Path. Define the Worth.**

One of the simplest but most powerful tricks I've learned is the reverse schedule. Start at the end. Visualize the outcome. What are you really trying to achieve? Be specific. Don't just say "success" or "freedom." Say "I want to launch a book that reaches fifty thousand readers." Or "I want to earn ten thousand dollars a month from my creative work." Get clear. Then, and only then, walk it back. Step by step. All the way to now.

Suddenly, that massive dream doesn't feel so abstract. The monster gets smaller. The fog starts to clear. You realize there's a logical path between where you are and where you want to be. Not magic. Not luck. Steps. Instead of staring at this overwhelming idea, "write a best-selling book", you break it down. Write the first draft. Edit. Send it to five friends. Select the ten best quotes. Build a landing page. Reach out to ten podcasts. Schedule launch content. Bit by bit, you build the staircase that leads to your outcome.

And here's the good news: everything becomes doable once you reframe it this way. You just need the right mindset. A clear map. And the refusal to quit.

But then comes the next question, the one that haunts creatives more than the blank page: "How do I get paid? How do I build wealth without selling my soul?" Let's be honest. We've been told that creatives suck at money. That artists can't price themselves. That writers should "just be grateful" to be published. That musicians shouldn't expect to be rich unless they're on a major label. This narrative is convenient, for consultants who want ten per cent of your earnings. For gatekeepers who thrive on your confusion.

You don't need to be a financial expert to set up systems that monetize your art. You need clarity, and courage. One rule I've come to love is the 10x Pricing Rule: stop charging based on a random chart or a freelancer forum. Charge based on impact. Charge for the value you bring, the clarity you offer, the energy you transfer, the years of experience behind each move.

If someone says "yes" to your price too quickly, you're probably too cheap. Think about Picasso. He once sketched a portrait in a matter of minutes, then charged a small fortune. Why? Because the client wasn't buying the ten minutes. They were buying the thirty years that made those ten minutes possible. The skill.

That's what pricing really reflects. Not your time, your story. So define your worth. Own your narrative. Protect your value, and stop apologizing for knowing what you bring to the table. This is how you build something sustainable. Something real.

### Structure the Journey: The Three-Tier Revenue Model

When you're sharing your work with the world, whether it's pitching a client, launching a product, or growing your audience, don't just showcase what you do. Structure it. Guide people through a path. One of the most effective ways to do that is to adopt the three-tier revenue model.

This model works because it creates clarity. Instead of firing arrows in all directions, you build a framework that meets your audience where they are, and invites them to move upward. Not with pressure. With progression.

Here's how it works:

- **Tier 1: Free Content**
  This is your visibility play. Your gift to the world. It might be articles, videos, podcast interviews, short guides, anything that provides value and opens the door. This is where people discover you. Where they realize you exist. It's how you build reach, not just recognition.

- **Tier 2: Low-Ticket Offer**
  This is your trust builder. Something accessible. A book, a workshop, a short course, a digital product, something that says: "I see you. Here's something valuable, without a big leap." It's low risk for them, high intention for you.

This is where conversion happens. Where interest becomes action.

- **Tier 3: High-Ticket Offer**
  This is your deep dive. Coaching, consulting, premium services, retreats, this is where transformation happens. Where your client or audience goes all in. You're not selling time. You're selling clarity. Direction. Depth. And the higher the value, the stronger the relationship becomes.

It's the same model your gym uses: free trial class, basic membership, private coaching. And it works, because it's natural. It mirrors how trust is built. First we try, then we commit. The beauty of this system isn't just in sales. It's in how it creates a journey. People aren't forced in. They're invited forward. And once they step in, that's when you shift your focus from conversion to retention. Because that's where long-term value lives.

And this is where a subscription model can become your greatest asset. Recurring income isn't reserved for tech bros and SaaS startups. You can build it, whether you're an illustrator, a writer, a filmmaker, or a creator of any kind. Tools like Patreon, Substack, or even app-integrated memberships give you the infrastructure. What matters is the intimacy you create. Done right, this isn't just about money. It's about belonging. It's a second family built around the work you love. A circle of people who don't just consume your work, they champion it. They stay for the long run. They grow with you. That's not just revenue but that's resonance.

By creating your work in different formats, like George Lucas did, you're not just producing content, you're building intellectual property. And today, IP is currency. With AI, Web3, and streaming platforms in constant search of original stories, your ideas are more valuable than ever. There are companies, real companies, whose sole job is to scout, license, and acquire IP. They're not looking for perfection. They're looking for potential.

So take a step back and ask yourself: what do you already own? What story, concept, character, or universe have you created that could live across different mediums? A short film can evolve into a graphic novel. A blog post can become a talk. A concept can expand into a world. The moment you realize your work is an asset, and not just output, you stop creating passively. You begin to think like a rights holder. Staking your IP means keeping your deck close and building long-term value. It's not about hoarding ideas or waiting ten years to release. It's about structuring what you already have, documenting it, protecting it, and thinking one step ahead. You are the foundation. And if you play smart, you stay in control.

The 30-30-30-10 Discipline: Build, Share, Learn, Connect. In your branding, the creative playbook is not optional. It's mandatory. Without it, you can quickly find yourself stuck, frustrated, scattered, and not getting the results you're after. You're doing the work, but somehow it's not landing. That's usually not because you're not talented. It's because your time isn't structured around what truly moves the needle.

One method I like to use is the 30-30-30-10 formula. No, it's not baby formula, it's a breakdown of how to spend your time if you're serious about building something that lasts. Thirty percent of your time should be spent creating. That's your core. That's where the magic happens. The second thirty percent? Marketing. Because what you create only matters if people actually see it. The next thirty per cent is for learning. Sharpening your edge. Staying alive mentally. And the final ten percent? Networking.

That last piece may surprise you. Some people put networking at the top of their list. I don't. I keep it at ten percent of my time, and I usually reserve it for the evening, when my creative energy is spent and I have more space for conversation. Not because I don't believe in connection. Quite the opposite. But I find most networking spaces to be emotionally exhausting. Mentally draining. A lot of the time, they feel like a post-work escape for people who aren't building anything real. That's not the energy I want to absorb.

When I network, I do it with intention. I'd rather have three meaningful one-on-one conversations than hand out twenty business cards I'll never follow up on. And truthfully, I've seen too many "networking" events filled with people orbiting around creativity without actually doing the work. I don't need to be in a room where inspiration is the currency and execution is absent. I want to be inspiring, not constantly trying to be inspired by people who are still waiting for permission.

That said, targeted networking, the kind where you know exactly who you want to connect with, and you do the research, the prep, and the outreach to make it happen, that's powerful. Sometimes, one connection really can change the game. Not because they'll save you, but because they open a door you didn't know was there. When that happens, it's not luck. It's alignment. It's preparation meeting the right person at the right time. Structure your time with clarity. Respect your energy. And don't let noise replace movement.

**Anchor the Brand: Build Your Flagship**

In brand building, one of the smartest moves you can make is to create a project that serves as your anchor. This is the piece that defines who you are. The one project that stands like a lighthouse in a sea of noise. It becomes your business card, your shorthand, your identity at a glance.

This is where everything we talked about around niche and focus comes together. Your flagship project is your DNA, crystallized. It's the most personal, the most aligned, the most essential thing you offer. Whether it's a brand, a work of art, a newsletter, a documentary, or a signature product, it needs to feel unmistakably you.

Once that's in place, you can communicate around it. You build stories around it. You share it, reference it, promote it, not because you're pushing, but because it's central. It becomes the center of gravity that all other content or offers orbit around.

In a world of infinite content and attention scarcity, this is how you create recognition. Not by screaming louder, but by standing firm on something clear. Because let's be honest, if you can't explain what you do in ten seconds, it's too vague. Vagueness doesn't convert. Clarity does. A lasting pitch needs to be impactful, precise, and bold. It doesn't need to say everything. It needs to say the right thing. Over time, this flagship becomes more than just a project. It becomes a standard, your internal quality benchmark, your external signature. You'll build your own creative playbook around it.

The tools I've given you here? They're just the foundation. Use them. Mix them with your personal rhythm, your lifestyle structure, your system of momentum and leverage.

Once your flagship is in place, very little can destabilize your machine. You're not at the mercy of platforms, trends, or algorithms. You're not being disrupted, you are the disruptor.

But of course, not everything is as sleek as it looks. Creativity, like any power, has a dark side. And if we're going to stay whole in this game, we need to face that too, clearly, consciously, and without fear.

# Chapter 6:

# The Dark Side of Creativity

There were moments I found myself banging my head against the wall, whispering over and over that I wasn't worth it. That I would never make anything happen. That nothing I touched would ever work. It was a time in my life when everything felt harder than it should've been. Every step forward felt like dragging a weight too heavy to carry. I was out of breath. Out of perspective. Walking a path where I was no longer kind to myself. I had become my own worst enemy. Every thought was dark. I wanted to disappear. Hide in a cave and wait for life to pass.

And then, I stopped.

That was the only life-saving action I could take. I stopped. I had been so entangled in my own obsessive need to create that I became toxic to myself. But strangely, I had to go through it. That darkness was part of my process. A necessary descent. A deep dive that brought clarity, insights, and a different kind of strength. Unmonitored, my creativity almost destroyed me. But once I applied my strategy, once I brought structure, purpose, and vision into the chaos, I became unbeatable.

Still, I will never forget that path. And neither should you.

My mom used to say, "Some things are free, but at some point, there's always something to pay." I didn't fully understand what she meant until I began working at the highest level of creative performance. Now I know exactly what she was talking about. Being creative is a gift. But applying it seriously, living it strategically, professionally, relentlessly, comes with a price.

There's a fine line between passion and obsession. And here's the paradox: you need obsession. Not a little spark here and there. Not occasional bursts of energy. You need a full, consuming, all-in obsession, right at the center of the frame. Without that, you can't embody your vision. You can't build something that moves people. You can't promote something you don't deeply believe in.

Obsession, on its own, isn't the villain. In fact, it's one of the most powerful fuels available. It sharpens your focus. It gets you in the zone. It unlocks flow states, long nights, and precision-level decisions. Obsession is what makes you care about every frame of your film, every line in your script, every sentence in your landing page. It's what allows you to reach that upper creative tier most people never touch.

But obsession left unchecked? That's where the danger lives. It starts slowly. You stop sleeping. You disconnect from people. You lose your sense of time, of rhythm, of why you started in the first place. Creativity becomes compulsion. You go from building something beautiful to becoming a prisoner of your own ambition.

It's like a financial bubble, think 2008. Everything looks good on the surface. Until it bursts. The crash doesn't just affect you. It affects your relationships. Everything: Your body, your health, your inner peace. That's why you have to stay brutally honest with yourself and your real priorities. If your family comes first, then act like it. Even when your brain is firing on all cylinders. Even when your fingers are twitching to answer one last message. If your kids are at the table, throw your phone across the room and be there fully. Because one day, they'll stop asking for your attention. And by then, it'll be too late. Unchecked obsession isn't noble. It's dangerous. And it can quietly destroy everything you're trying to build.

Being creative is incredible. It's rare. It's powerful. You are one of those people. That's why you must protect the very thing that allows you to create. You need obsession, but only if it's paired with clarity. Don't let the thing that fuels you consume you.

**The Weight of Sacrifice**

Sacrifices are part of the game. And they're okay, as long as you're at peace with them. You won't be able to do it all, even if you want to. That's not how life works. Something always gets left behind. And that's not failure. That's the focus. The sooner you accept this, the less you'll suffer. If you fight it, you'll hit a wall, mentally, emotionally, and physically. But if you accept it with clarity, sacrifice becomes fuel. It becomes proof that you're making space for something greater.

Sacrifices mean choosing. They mean creating room to fully pursue what your vision is asking of you. For me, that meant leaving Los Angeles and moving back to Provence. But long before that, it meant leaving Provence for New York. I was twenty-two. I didn't even have a clear vision yet, just a gut instinct that where I was didn't match who I wanted to become. So I left. Doing so, I left behind my family, my closest friends, a girlfriend I cared about. I stepped into the unknown with nothing but hunger.

Twelve years later, I returned. I came back to a different version of everything I had left behind. My family had aged. The person I'd loved was no longer there. And in returning, I also walked away from something else: a working system in Los Angeles. A network, my community. A city that made sense for the kind of career I was building. But I had changed. My vision had evolved. I wanted to raise my son here. I wanted peace, depth, soil, and presence.

That's the truth about sacrifice. It's not just about giving things up. It's about choosing what matters more. It's about being willing to let go of good things for the right reasons. And when you do that, those sacrifices stop feeling like losses. They become checkpoints. Markers of growth. Signs that you were moving with intention.

The real danger isn't in what you leave behind, it's in the regret you carry if you don't own your choices. Regret is heavy. It sticks and doesn't hesitate to poison progress. So when you make a decision, especially the big ones, make sure it's truly yours. Not driven by fear. Not shaped by someone else's opinion. Yours. That way, no matter how things turn out, you'll never end up blaming anyone else.

And that's freedom.

That's alignment.

That's the quiet strength of a life lived on your terms.

## The Burnout Spiral

There are a lot of geniuses out there who experience burnout. People with vision, drive, and depth crushed under the weight of their own momentum. I say that because I've been there. I've lived it. For a long time, I struggled with it, watching the obsession inside me slowly devour whatever strength I had left. And it didn't happen all at once. It crept in quietly. Until one day, I realized I wasn't okay. I was sad all the time. My heart felt bitter. And no matter how much I worked, I couldn't find any sweetness in it anymore. I was drained, not just physically, but emotionally. There were many reasons I felt that way at the time, circumstances, relationships, pressure, but when I cut through the noise, one thing stood out above all the rest: I wasn't driven by the right reason.

I was chasing. Chasing approval. Chasing success. Chasing relevance. Locked into this treadmill of constant motion, where the only reward was the next deadline. The next pitch. The next appearance of progress. I was moving without moving, working without breathing. And every time I created, it wasn't because I wanted to, it was because I had to. Because if I stopped, I might disappear. That's how it felt. That's the real danger. When you push so hard for something that once made you feel alive, it's frighteningly easy to drift. To lose touch with what made you fall in love with it in the first place. You start performing instead of creating. Delivering instead of dreaming. You strip the joy from your art. You turn play into pressure. And that transformation? It's subtle. But when it lands, it lands hard.

That's where burnout lives. In the quiet space between your obsession and your purpose. When the balance breaks, everything that once lifted you begins to crush you. And it hurts. More than most people are willing to admit. Because it's not just exhaustion. It's grief.

You're grieving the thing you used to love. The part of yourself you buried to keep producing.

If you've been there, you know what I mean. If you're in it now, let this be your reminder: it's not a weakness to feel it. It's not a failure. But it is a signal. A call to pause, to reset, and to return, not to some perfect version of yourself, but to the one who started all this in the first place. The one who dreamed. The one who played. The one who smiled while building. Burnout doesn't mean you're broken. It means something inside you is asking to be heard.

## Sanity and the Creative Mind

There is a real relationship between creativity and madness. And I'm not saying that being a creative person makes you unstable, but creativity, when taken seriously, when pursued with honesty, forces you to go deep. It pulls you inward, into places most people avoid. Places that hurt. That's the nature of the work. Even the best strategist, when they go fully into the process, ends up exposed. Vulnerable. Raw. It's like standing naked in the open, exhilarating and terrifying at the same time.

One day you're full of energy, the next you're exhausted. One day it's coffee, the next it's tea. The contrast is constant. With that fluctuation comes sensitivity. A creative mind is often a sensitive mind, open to nuance, emotion, and tension. That's a strength. But it also comes with risk. The more attuned you are to what's real, the more you feel. And feeling, when not managed with care, can spiral fast.

We often romanticize the genius. But the truth is, the true creative isn't a genius in the traditional sense, they're simply someone who accesses a part of the mind that becomes more vulnerable to thoughts, impulses, and moods. That's where the shadow creeps in. What people sometimes call self-destruction isn't about drama or attention. It's about reaching a threshold. Acting against your best interest, not because you want to, but because you're overwhelmed by something bigger than you.

This is where strategy meets psychology. You're not a therapist. But if you want to play the long game, if you want to create without burning out, build without breaking down, you need to understand the space you're operating in. And that means setting up systems not just for output, but for mental health. You need to build a safety valve.

For some, that's running through canyons. For others, it's boxing. Or swimming. Driving. Surfing. Breathing. For me, it's the stars. After a shoot, after a long sprint, I stop. I slow everything down. I go outside. I reconnect with whatever grounds me. It sounds simple, and it is. But it's also essential. Because that ritual is what keeps me sane.

Whatever it is for you, protect it. Don't sacrifice it. Don't brush it aside as optional. That's your internal compass. Your anchor. And when you're performing at the highest level, when the stakes are high and the stakes are you, staying sane isn't luxury, it's non-negotiable.

You want to perform like a master? Start by protecting the one doing the performing. Know the traps. Expect them. But don't surrender to them.

Your safe haven is what makes the whole thing possible.

# Epilogue:

# The Message I Never Got

What you just read is a scream from my heart. It's the message I wish someone had whispered to me when I was alone in the wild, forgotten, confused, lost, unsure of what to build or where to aim. It's the light I needed when everyone around me said it wasn't possible. That being creative meant being broke. That artists were destined to starve. That dreams were for later, for others, for after.

Yes, this book is a toolkit. A system, but beyond that, it's a reminder. A reminder that you're not alone. That the way you feel, the doubt, the chaos, the fire, is universal. That even the most accomplished creators walk through darkness. That creativity isn't a rare gift reserved for a chosen few. It's human. It's alive in all of us. Our story is our most important tool, to nurture preciously. I'm not here to educate. I'm here to give. To tell you: you're not crazy for wanting more. You're not arrogant for believing your ideas matter. You're not naïve for thinking art can change the world. Our stories sit at the center of our lives. We no longer dig coal mines. We dig into ourselves. We shape meaning. We give form to the invisible. We are a generation with infinite tools, infinite platforms, infinite access. And yet what matters most has never changed: the courage to show up with truth.

I truly believe everyone is an artist. And if that word feels too heavy, too foreign, too big, replace it. Say creator. Say builder. Say human. It doesn't matter. What matters is this: you carry something. Something powerful. Something only you can give.

So have fun. Go explore. Make messes. Fall in love with process. With questions. With beauty. With rage. Keep in mind that what will take you the furthest... is what you love the most.

Be excited.
Be curious.
Own your story.

You have the strength to change everything. And you are worth it.

**Farewell.**

# Exercises:

Before you move forward, take the time to apply everything you've absorbed.
Theory alone won't shift your world. Action will.
These exercises are designed to help you think, feel, and move like a true creative strategist.
Do them with honesty. Revisit them often. Let them grow with you.

# Chapter 1: Forge Your Creative Identity

### 1. The Artist Legacy Statement

**Prompt:** Imagine it's twenty years from now. Your career has taken its full shape.
What would you want your creative legacy to be remembered for?

**Action:**
Write a short statement (5–10 sentences) that captures what you stood for, what you created,

and what you changed.

Be specific.

Don't write what you think people expect.

Write what you would be proud of.

**Example start:**

*"I built a creative empire based on authenticity and storytelling that challenged conventional norms..."*

## 2. The Perception Challenge

**Prompt:** How are you currently perceived by others?

How do you want to be perceived?

**Action:**

In two columns, write:

- On the left: Three adjectives people might use to describe your work today.

- On the right: Three adjectives you want people to use about your work and presence in the future.

Identify the gap. Choose one practical action you can take this month to align your real-world presence with your inner vision.

### 3. The Mental Model Artist

**Prompt:** What mental models or systems guide the way you create today?
How intentional are you about them?

**Action:**

List 3 mental models you want to consciously adopt in your creative process.
(Ex: "Scarcity creates value," "Story is emotion first," "Momentum beats perfection.")

Describe in a few sentences how you will integrate each model into your actual daily or weekly work.
Not theoretical, practical.

**Advanced Challenge: The Creative Strategist's Sprint**

**Optional for those who want to go further.**

Over the next 7 days:

- Create something every single day (even if it's small).

- Share at least one piece publicly (social media, portfolio, network).

- Reflect in a journal for 5 minutes daily: What worked? What didn't? What energized you?

At the end of 7 days, review everything you created. Identify what felt most alive, and double down on it for the next month.

Becoming a creative strategist is not a moment. It's a movement. And it begins here, with the deliberate decision to claim your voice, your vision, and your discipline.

The world needs what you have to offer.
Let's build it, one move at a time.

# Chapter 2: Build Your Creative Foundation

The exercises that follow are not meant to entertain you, they are meant to shake you awake. They are designed to force you to confront yourself honestly, to raise your standards, and to step into the version of you that builds, creates, and leads.

If you skip them, you will stay the same. If you do them, you will start to shift. This is where theory ends and real work begins. Grab a notebook, block out time, and take this seriously. Your future self will thank you.

### 1. The Mirror Rule

Your life mirrors the standards you set for yourself. If you want to change your reality, you must first raise your standards.

- **List 3 creatives you admire deeply.**
  Not just for their success, but for their
  way of living, their work ethic, their
  mindset. For each one, identify what
  you think their standards are. How do
  they treat their craft? How do they treat
  themselves?

- **Now, turn the mirror toward yourself.**
  List 3 areas of your life where you
  currently tolerate mediocrity. Be
  brutally honest. This is not about guilt,
  it's about clarity.

- **Write a creative contract to yourself.**
  On one page, set your new standards.
  Declare clearly what you no longer
  tolerate and what you commit to
  raising. Sign it. Date it. Pin it
  somewhere you will see every day.

## 2. The Creative Audit

Before building something strong, you need to know exactly where you stand.

- **Write down your current creative projects or dreams.**
  Be specific. No "I want to write more." Write "Finish first draft of my novel by" or "Publish a photography portfolio by October."

- **Assess your current level of action toward each one.**
  Rate from 0 to 10 how much consistent action you're taking (not thinking, not planning but action).

- **Ask yourself:**
  Where am I still stuck in motion rather than true action?
  What one small action could I take this week to move forward by even one per cent?

## 3. Manifestation and Silence Challenge

- **Declare one goal aloud to someone you trust.**
  Choose a project that truly matters to you. State your commitment clearly and simply.

- **For the next 7 days, practice strategic silence.**
  No useless debates. No constant justifications. Save your voice for your work and for manifesting.

## 4. Bonus Exercise: The Burn List

Sometimes, we need to consciously let go to move forward.

- **Write down a list of distractions, excuses, and time-wasters** that currently slow you down. Include habits, people, mindsets, everything.

- **Burn the list (safely).**
  Literally or symbolically. Let it go. Clear the space for your real work.

If you did these exercises honestly, you now have a mirror in front of you. You see your strengths. You see your weaknesses. You see your excuses. And you see your potential.

No one is coming to build your creative life for you. But now, you hold the blueprint, and the pen.
Every change you want starts with a first act of commitment. These exercises are that first act.

# Chapter 3: Building Your Empire

These exercises are designed to push you into real movement. No shortcuts, no wishful thinking, only real steps toward building the creative empire you envision.

Take your time. Be honest. And most importantly, act.

## 1. Who Is in Your Inner Circle?

List the five people you spend the most time with (in real life or online). Next to each name, answer honestly:

- Are they pulling me upward or holding me back?

- Do they challenge me to grow, or do they feed my comfort zone?

- Would I want to become more like them?

Once you're done, ask yourself: what needs to change?
You don't have to cut ties with everyone overnight. But you do have to protect your energy and choose your proximity wisely.

## 2. Identify a Bigger Player in Your Field and Reach Out

Pick one person in your field you admire, someone a few steps ahead of you. Not a celebrity, not someone completely unreachable, but a real player doing real work.

- Research them carefully. Understand what they stand for.

- Craft a genuine, thoughtful question. (Not "Can I pick your brain?" but something specific: "What helped you the most during your first product launch?" / "What book shifted your creative career the most?" etc.)

Now send the message. The act of reaching out will already shift your mindset from passive to active.

### 3. The Gold Seed Vision

Take 15 minutes to answer the following:

- What is one "gold seed" you want to plant for the next 5 years? (A project, a business, a body of work.)

- Why does it matter to you?

- What tiny first step can you take this week to move toward planting it?

Write it down. Be clear. Be bold. Even if it feels ridiculous. Especially if it feels ridiculous.

Your empire won't appear by magic. It will be built one connection, one decision, one gold seed at a time.

The sooner you start moving, the sooner your vision stops being just a dream, and starts becoming your reality.

# Chapter 4: Storytelling That Resonates

You're not here to play the algorithm. You're here to connect. These exercises are here to help you stop guessing, and start speaking to the right people, the right way.

Don't skip them. This is where the real shift happens.

## 1. Audience Deep Dive. Who Are You Really Speaking To?

Describe your ideal audience. Not in general terms. Be specific.

- What are they struggling with right now?

- What do they secretly hope for?

- What kind of content do they love, and why?

- What keeps them scrolling? What stops them cold?

- What makes them say "this was made for me"?

Now go deeper:

- Where do they spend time online?

- Who do they follow? What do they comment on?

- What language do they use when they talk about their challenges?

- If they met you today, what would they need to hear to feel seen?

Optional twist: write one open letter to this person. No sales, no pitch. Just the truth. Let them know you see them.

## 2. Identity Connection. What Story Are You Really Telling?

Every brand, every artist, every voice carries an identity, whether you choose it or not.
Let's make yours intentional.

- What are three words people should associate with your presence?

- What are three truths you refuse to compromise on?

- What kind of transformation are you inviting your audience into?

- What does someone become by being in your world?

Now, look at your current content, your posts, bios, messages. Are they aligned? If not: what needs to shift?

Bonus: choose one sentence that captures your brand's inner truth. Write it, and memorize it. Return to it often.

### 3. Build Your Resonance Map (optional but powerful)

Take a blank sheet. Divide it in two:

- **Left side**: What you want to say

- **Right side**: What they need to hear

Match them. Find the bridge. That's your storytelling sweet spot. Don't aim to speak to everyone. Aim to matter to the right ones. When you stop shouting into the void and start whispering with precision, the right people hear you loud and clear.

# Chapter 5: The Creative playbook

This chapter gave you structure. But none of it matters unless you make it your own. These exercises aren't here to impress you, they're here to activate you. To turn what you just read into something that lives in your calendar, your habits, and your bottom line. Take the time. Go deep. No one is watching, but your future self will thank you.

### 1. Evaluate Yourself

Rate yourself from 1 to 10 in the following key areas:

- **Business Acumen**: Do you understand the mechanics of value creation, positioning, and offer design?

- **Execution Discipline**: Are you showing up consistently and getting things done without waiting for inspiration?

- **Influence**: Do people understand what you stand for? Are you actively shaping perception?

- **Audience Growth**: Are you reaching new people each month? Are you turning attention into engagement?

Now reflect:
What's your strongest area? What needs the most work?
Choose one to focus on this month and outline 3 concrete actions to improve.

## 2. Reverse Engineering

Start with your end goal. It can be a book, a company, a film, a show, a brand, whatever is most alive for you.
Write it down in one clear sentence. Now work

backwards. List at least 10 specific steps between today and that goal. Don't worry about the perfect order. What matters is clarity of direction.

Highlight the first 2 steps you can take this week.

**3. Your Playbook Recap**

Take a moment to summarize your system.
What are your 3 main creative pillars?
(projects, offers, formats)
What's your 30-30-30-10 split for this month?
What's your current daily sprint routine?
 Where do you need to simplify or remove friction?

Use this as your living system. Refine it each month.

**4. Structure Your Day**

Design a week that reflects your creative rhythm.
Choose a theme for each day (Creation / Execution / Outreach / Rest / Strategy, etc.)

Block a non-negotiable daily sprint time.
Assign no more than two big goals per week.
Then ask yourself:
Is this structure supporting your energy, or draining it? Adjust accordingly.

### 5. Monetize Smartly

Think about your current offers, or potential ones.
Draft your Three-Tier Revenue Model:

- Free (visibility)

- Low-ticket (trust builder)

- High-ticket (transformation)

Can you add a recurring/subscription layer?
How are you currently pricing your work? Is it aligned with your impact?

Now write one sentence that affirms your new creative standard: "I charge based on the value I bring, not the hours I spend."

You now have a personal playbook, one that reflects your vision, your rhythm, your priorities. But a playbook isn't just something you write once and forget. It's a living system, meant to grow with you. Return to it often. Refine it when necessary. And remember: this isn't about doing more. It's about doing what matters, consistently. You're not just building projects. You're building your creative empire. One move at a time.

## Chapter 6: The Shadow Work

This chapter wasn't meant to scare you. It was meant to ground you. To remind you that creativity, obsession, vulnerability, and burnout often live in the same house. You don't need to fix yourself, you need to observe yourself. These exercises are here to deepen your awareness, not judge your rhythm. Take them seriously. Take your time. This is part of the work too.

## 1. The Shadow of Reflection

Take a quiet moment and write your answers to the following questions:

- What have you sacrificed lately to pursue your vision?

- Were those sacrifices conscious or reactive?

- What's something you used to love, but now feels heavy or forced?

- What's the price of your current pace, emotionally, physically, relationally?

Finish with this:
"If I keep going like this for 6 more months, I will..."
Write honestly. Then ask: is that where I want to be?

## 2. The Dark Fuel Exercise

We all have a hidden engine, something dark
we draw energy from. Maybe it's anger. Maybe
it's a need to prove someone wrong. Maybe it's
fear of being invisible. Write down the fuel that
pushes you when nothing else works.
Where does it come from?
Is it sustainable?
Can it be transformed into something
healthier, without losing your edge?

Now write a short statement:
"I no longer need to suffer to create. I can build
from clarity, not from chaos." Say it out loud.

## 3. Build Your Safe Haven

List the rituals or actions that help you feel like
yourself again when everything spins out of
control.

- Is it a walk, a workout, silence, music,
  cooking, nature? List at least three
  non-negotiables you can come back to
  regularly. Now schedule them. Literally.

One per week for the next month.
Protect that time.

## 4. Burnout Awareness Scale

From 1 to 10, rate the following:

- Sleep quality

- Joy in your creative process

- Sense of clarity

- Time for recovery

- Desire to create (not out of pressure)

Write one thing you can stop doing this week.
And one thing you can start doing to feel
better.

## Before you go

You've made it to the end. But this isn't the end. You've excavated the truth. Named what you buried.

Felt what they told you to hide. You've shaped a story no one else could write.

That is no small thing. And now? Now you walk with it. You speak from it.

You share it, not to impress, but to connect. Not to perform, but to lead.

This story won't fix everything. But it will open doors. It will protect your voice from erasure.

It will remind you who you are when the noise gets loud again.

You don't need permission anymore. Only courage. And rhythm.

So go. Not louder. But deeper. Your story is ready. And the world is listening.

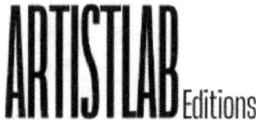

**ARTISTLAB** Editions

We're here to crack open the doors of screenwriting and let the real stuff breathe. The truth is, most screenplays are locked away, hoarded by a handful of insiders who keep the craft guarded and obscure. We're not doing that. We're putting it all out there.

Why? Because screenwriting is a powerful craft. It's raw, it's relentless, and it's too important to be kept under lock and key. We're digging up the classics, the gems that still burn bright, and the fresh voices cutting through the noise to build a compelling collection.

We're about access, giving aspiring writers, filmmakers, and passionate readers the tools to learn from the best. To dive deep into their techniques, their rhythms, their structure. To break down the beats that make stories hit hard and stick. It's about taking what works, discarding what doesn't, and building something entirely new.

This is more than just publishing. It's a movement. A dedication to the art of storytelling that goes beyond the finished film. Whether it's a timeless classic or a bold new voice, our curated selection is here to inspire, educate, and challenge the way you see storytelling.

This isn't just about reading scripts, it's about the essence of storytelling. About giving artists the tools to break rules, bend formats, and make something that matters. Because stories aren't just words on a page, they're blueprints we create.

Artist Lab Editions. Where writers rise.